WHO'S THE DADDY?

DADDY?

JOKE BOOK

Published in Great Britain in 2008 by
Prion
an imprint of the
Carlton Publishing Group
20 Mortimer Street
London W1T 3JW

1 3 5 7 9 10 8 6 4 2

Text copyright © 2008 Mike Haskins and Clive Whichelow
Design and layout copyright © 2008 Carlton Books Ltd

ISBN 978-1-85375-655-9

Typeset by E-Type, Liverpool
Printed and bound in Great Britain by Mackays

WHO'S THE
DADDY?
JOKE BOOK

Jokes, stories and all sorts of
funny stuff to do with dads

Mike Haskins & Clive Whichelow

PRION

INTRODUCTION

I t's a tough life being a dad isn't it? You've got all the
responsibility and none of the power. Nominally, of course,
you're the head of the household, but try telling that to the
rest of the family who, when they're not spending your money
or eating you out of house and home, are wrecking the place
or demanding new this and new that – and we won't even
mention the other.

You spend all day at work providing for the ungrateful so-
and-sos and when you come home you can't even watch your
favourite TV programme because either the kids are watching
endless cartoons or the wife is catching up on the soaps. Even
the cat's sitting in your best chair.

Eventually, you get the kids to bed, have something to
eat and settle down for the evening, finding that you've got
approximately two hours before it's time to start getting ready
for bed. This brief period of respite is broken up by the wife
dropping hints about little jobs that need doing round the house
or yet another list of things she's found to spend your money on.

But there's always the weekend isn't there? Ah yes, the
weekend. This, in theory, is what you spend your whole week
working for: rest, relaxation and the chance to do those things
you've been looking forward to all week, such as playing golf,
going to the pub, watching sport on TV, or just mooching
around the house after a leisurely lie-in and doing nothing
in particular. Dream on! One of the kids has to go to ballet
classes, the other one is doing martial arts, the wife wants to go
shopping, the garden needs weeding and the gas man is arriving
"any time between eight a.m. and the fifth of March next year".
In addition to this the car has been making a "funny noise" and

needs looking at, and the cat, who has done nothing all week but laze around on your favourite chair, seems to be off his food but has nevertheless been sick over your carpet and now needs taking to the vet.

By the end of the weekend you're absolutely knackered and, quite frankly, rather warming to the idea of getting back to work. At least there you're paid to be worked like a horse and treated like a dog. But it's not always like that is it? No, let's not exaggerate. There are those moments when the wife brings you an unexpected cup of tea or when the kids are playing quietly in their own room and you have a few minutes of blissful peace. Unfortunately, Father's Day only comes once a year.

What Is A Dad?

A father is a man with pictures in his wallet, where he used to keep his money when he was single.

"A father is a banker provided by nature."
French proverb

"Becoming a father is easy enough, but being one can be very rough."
Wilhelm Busch

"[Having children] is an affirmation of manhood in the eyes of the world. A man needs to establish to his society that he is a man. He could just go around showing his genitals to people. Many men do, indeed, opt for this course of action."
Jeremy Hardy

"When you're a dad you can wear huge pants. Huge dad-sized underpants. Where do dads get their pants? They're vast! 'Look at my pants! I'm a dad! I've got my car in there! I have an acre of pants!' Go to Marks and Spencer: 'Packet of three parachute pants please!'"
Alan Davies

Eddy: Family? Family?! God I hope you
     haven't invited that bloody, bollocky, selfish,
     two-faced, chicken, bastard, pig-dog man
     have you?
Saffy: You could just say "Dad".
                                    Absolutely Fabulous

"Fatherhood is pretending the present you
love most is soap-on-a-rope."
                                    Bill Cosby

"Why are men reluctant to become fathers?
They aren't through being children."
                                    Cindy Garner

"You don't have to deserve your mother's
love. You have to deserve your father's. He's
more particular."
                                    Robert Frost

A small boy gets lost at the funfair and has to find a policeman.
"I've lost my daddy," he tells the policeman. "OK," says the
policeman, "I'll help you find him. First I'll need a description.
So what's your father like?" The kid thinks for a moment then
says, "Beer and women."

Dad asks his young son, "Do you know what Father's Day is?"
"Yes," says the boy, "it's exactly the same as Mother's Day but
you don't have to spend as much."

There are three stages in a man's life: first he believes in Father
Christmas, next he doesn't believe in Father Christmas, finally he
finds he is Father Christmas.

Daddy arrives back home one day with a huge packet of sweets.
He gathers his children around and says, "OK. These sweeties
are going to the person here who never answers Mummy back
and who always does what Mummy tells them. So who should

have them?" And the kids look at him and say together, "You should."

"One father is more than a hundred schoolmasters."

English Proverb

"Fathers are the geniuses of the house because only a person as intelligent as us could fake such stupidity. Think about your father. He doesn't know where anything is. You ask him to do something, he messes it up and your mother sends you: "Go down and see what your father's doing before he blows up the house." He's a genius at work because he doesn't want to do it, and he knows someone will be coming soon to stop him."

Bill Cosby

"I cannot think of any need in childhood as strong as the need for a father's protection."

Sigmund Freud

"I'm a white male, age 18 to 49. Everyone listens to me, no matter how dumb my suggestions are."

Homer Simpson

"The one thing that all men seek from a child is a renewal of their own lives. Perhaps we all want a little replica of ourselves and becoming a father is an easier way of doing this than becoming a major historical figure in order to be included in the Airfix range."

Jeremy Hardy

Are You A Traditional Dad Or A Modern Dad?

Once upon a time if a baby opened its eyes in the cot and saw someone with blonde highlighted hair and earrings it would probably be its mother. Now it's just as likely to be its father. Which one are you?

Traditional dads can change a plug but not a nappy; modern Dads can change a nappy but try to avoid it in case they sully their designer jeans.

Traditional dads wouldn't attend a birth if you paid them; modern dads not only attend it, they jump into the birthing pool to be at one with the mother and quite frankly get in the flipping way.

Traditional dads would come home from work and give the kids a good thrashing; modern dads come home from work and give the kids a good thrashing on the PlayStation.

Traditional dads helped kids with homework; modern dads, due to modern teaching methods, have less idea than their kids how to do it.

Traditional dads played "Cowboys and Indians" with their kids; modern dads won't let children have toy guns because of "negative conditioning," and wouldn't dream of insulting "native Americans" in this way.

Traditional dads come home and expect to see their dinner on the table; modern dads never have dinner at a table.

Traditional dads had blue-collar jobs and worked down the pit; modern dads think blue-collar jobs are the pits.

Traditional dads would have to fork out for the wife's visits to the hairdresser; modern dads have to fork out for their own visits to the hairdresser.

Traditional dads would bring home a bunch of flowers if they stayed too long at the pub; modern dads get a bunch of fives if they stay too long at the pub.

Traditional dads just didn't understand women; modern dads think they understand women, but they still don't.

Dad's Impossible Role Models

Batman – let's face it, you're never going to have a cool car that zooms out of an underground cave in a cloud of dust before you go and catch a few colourful villains and get home in time to sort out the evening's homework.

David Beckham – he's cool, he plays football, he's rich, good looking and he has a better haircut than you. How on earth are you expected to compete? On the other hand, it's difficult to believe Victoria ever serves him up with a decent meal, isn't it?

The dad from *Home Alone* – every child's dream: the father who takes the rest of the family off on holiday and leaves his little boy to his own devices, i.e. the important things in life such as ordering home delivery pizza, eating sweets, and catching burglars in a variety of amusing ways. It's got to be more fun than going to some crummy holiday apartment with the rest of your sad family, hasn't it?

Father Christmas – the daddy of them all. He's the man with all the toys, as the song says. Yeah, grumpy old Dad manages to fork out for a couple of presents at Yuletide, but Santa, he doesn't worry about the cost, he just goes right ahead and fills up that stocking with goodies galore and makes you look like a cheapskate. Cheers Santa.

Genghis Khan – according to scientific studies he didn't just rule the largest empire in the world, he helped populate it as well. Eight per cent of men living in the area that was once the Mongol Empire are directly descended from him. This translates into 0.5 per cent of the entire male population of the world today. Well, if Dad is Genghis' son and heir that at least explains his bad temper.

Darth Vader – managed to keep the fact that he was Luke Skywalker's dad a secret until the very last moment of his life. Where was the Child Support Agency on that case?

Mulai Ismail (1646–1727) the last Sharifian Emperor of Morocco – according to some sources the most prolific dad in history. Reports say that by 1703 he had sired at least 342 daughters and 525 sons and was by then looking extremely tired and had to walk everywhere with his legs bent slightly outwards. According to less reliable historical sources, he was the recipient of so many unimaginative Father's Day presents every year, he attempted to offload them by founding the Sock Shop chain in 1704.

God the Father – set a slightly high standard as regards the number of little jobs that dads should be able to get done around the place in less than seven days.

Dad Through The Ages

Four years old: "My daddy can do anything!"

Seven years old: "My dad knows a lot... a whole lot."

Eight years old: "My father does not know quite everything."

Twelve years old: "Oh well, naturally Father does not know that either."

Fourteen years old: "My dad? He's a bit old fashioned."

Twenty-one years old: "My dad is completely out of date!"

Twenty-five years old: "My old man knows a little bit about it, but not much."

Thirty years old: "Hmm. I must ask Dad and sees what he thinks about it."

Thirty-five years old: "Before we decide, we will get Dad's opinion on things."

Fifty years old: "Damn it! What would Dad have thought about this?"

Sixty years old: "My old dad was an incredible fellow. He knew literally everything!"

Sixty-five years old: "You know what, I wish I could talk it over with Dad once more."

All About Dad

Eddie's parents worked in a fairground. His mum was a clairvoyant and his dad was a contortionist. As a result, Eddie was born with the uncanny ability to foresee his own end.

"Someone told me I should tell my dad I love him before he dies... but what if I get the timing wrong and he lives for another 20 years?! I don't think either of us could deal with the embarrassment! I'd have to kill him!"
Ardal O'Hanlon

"[On meeting aliens] Please don't eat me! I have a wife and kids. Eat them!"
Homer Simpson

"When I was a boy of 14, my father was so ignorant I could hardly stand to have the old man around. But when I got to be 21, I was astonished at how much he had learned in seven years."
Mark Twain

"When I was ten, my pa told me never to talk to strangers. We haven't spoken since."
Steven Wright

"I was raised by just my mom. See, my father died when I was eight years old. At least, that's what he told us in the letter."
Drew Carey

"Just because I don't care doesn't mean I don't understand."
Homer Simpson

"If I turn into my parents, I'll either be an alcoholic blonde chasing after 20-year-old boys or... I'll end up like my mom."
Chandler Bing/ Friends

"If it weren't biologically impossible, I'd swear that Dad was dropped in a basket on our doorstep."
Frasier

George Burns: Are you the oldest in the family?
Gracie Allen: No, no, my mother and father are much older.

The Burns And Allen Show

"My father confused me. From the ages of one to seven, I thought my name was Jesus Christ!"

Bill Cosby

"Advice from a small child: when your dad is really angry, if he asks you, "Do I look stupid?" don't answer."

Nine-year-old girl

"My dad used to say, "always fight fire with fire," which is probably why he got thrown out of the fire brigade."

Harry Hill

"My dad is Irish and my mum is Iranian, which meant that we spent most of our family holidays in Customs."

Patrick Monahan

"My father hated radio and he could not wait for television to be invented so that he could hate that too."

Peter De Vries

"Nobody ever asks a father how he manages to combine marriage and a career."

Sam Ewing

"Even though your kids will consistently do the exact opposite of what you're telling them to do, you have to keep loving them just as much."

Bill Cosby

"Happy is the father whose child finds his attempts to amuse it, amusing."

Robert Lynd

"I don't apologize. I am sorry Lisa, that's the way I am."

Homer Simpson

"If the new American father feels bewildered and even defeated, let him take comfort from the fact that whatever he does in any fathering situation has a 50 per cent chance of being right."

Bill Cosby

"I am an expert of electricity. My father occupied the chair of applied electricity at the state prison."

WC Fields

"My childhood should have taught me lessons for my own fatherhood, but it didn't because parenting can only be learned by people who have no children."

Bill Cosby

"My father used to play the tuba as a young man. He tried to play the tuba, he tried to play 'Flight of the Bumblebee', and blew his liver out through the horn."

Woody Allen

"By the time a man realizes that maybe his father was right he usually has a son who thinks he's wrong!"

Charles Wadsworth

"Well, it's one a.m. Better go home and spend some quality time with the kids."

Homer Simpson

Special Features Dad Dreams Of
Installing In His Car

A taxi-style dividing window between the front and rear seats with which he can silence squabbling kids at a stroke.

Ejector seats just in case the above isn't effective enough.

An in-car toilet so he doesn't have to keep stopping on motorways because one of the kids is "desperate!"

A meter for charging teenage children who have to be picked up drunk from city centres at all hours.

A reassuring feminine sat-nav voice that constantly tells him he's doing a great job even if the rest of the family don't think so, he's a wonderful dad etc. etc.

An "automatic pilot" switch that takes over when he wants to sit back and relax for a change.

A sweets dispenser to pacify kids on long journeys.

A special sat-nav-style voice that points out all the horses, cows, sheep and tractors to young children so he doesn't have to do it.

A mini-fridge so he can have a quiet beer while Mum's driving.

Becoming A Dad

I n theory, you've got the best half of the bargain. You don't have to walk round with a stomach the size of a space hopper for nine months (unless you also happen to be either a professional darts player or indeed a space hopper). You don't have to go through the agonies of childbirth, and you don't have to lay off the booze and fags or suffer the indignities of public breastfeeding.

But! Who is it that has to do the fetching and carrying while her nibs is having afternoon naps or having to watch what she lifts? Who is it that has to run her around for appointments at the clinic/chiropodist/aromatherapist for months on end? Who is it that nearly has a heart seizure every time she has a false alarm and thinks he's going to have to deliver the baby himself at home?

That's right, you, you poor sod. But do you get any sympathy? No. The missus is the one everyone feels sorry for. You're about as important as a toilet roll. Everyone takes you for granted and only notices you if you run out. And you can't do that can you? You've got to be there round the clock, solid, dependable and supportive, offering a kind word, a listening ear, and the occasional mop and bucket.

But then the big day finally comes, and there you are at the side of the hospital bed: the proudest day of your life as you hold her hand, mop her brow and get sworn at for several hours on end. But it's all worth it eventually. Out pops this little bundle of loveliness, this miracle of life, this beautiful little baby that you helped to produce.

But everyone forgets that don't they? Who gets all the credit? She does. When was the last time you heard of a dad getting bunches of flowers and boxes of chocolates for their efforts?

Still, it's good preparation for life as a dad – get used to it.

> **"I said, 'Darling, I'll be a great father. I'll be there at the birth and everything.' She said, 'John, I don't want you there at the conception.'"**
> **John Dowie**

A man knocks on his boss's door. "Hi, boss," he says, "Is there any chance I could have next week off because my wife and I are expecting a baby?" "Really?" says the boss, "Of course. When's it due?" "Well," says the man, "that depends, but hopefully in about nine months and one week's time."

> **"We had our first child on the NHS. It was absolutely terrible. We had to wait nine months."**
>
> *A Bit of Fry and Laurie*

A man is waiting for his wife to give birth. The doctor comes in and informs the father that his son was born without torso, arms or legs. The son is just a head! But the father loves his son and raises him as well as he can, with love and compassion. After 18 years, the son is old enough for his first drink. The father takes him to the bar and tearfully tells the son he is proud of him whilst ordering up the biggest, strongest drink for his boy. With all the regulars looking on curiously and the barman shaking his head in disbelief, the boy takes his first sip of alcohol. Swoooop! A torso pops out! The bar is dead silent; then bursts into a whoop of joy. The father, shocked, begs his son to drink again. The regulars chant, "Take another drink!" The barman still shakes his head in dismay. Swoooop! Two arms pop out. The bar goes wild. The father, crying and wailing, begs his son to drink again. The regulars chant, "Take another drink!" The barman ignores the whole affair. By now the boy is getting tipsy, and with his new hands he reaches down, grabs his drink and guzzles the last of it. Swoooop! Two legs pop out. The bar is in chaos. The father thanks God. The boy stands up on his new legs and stumbles to the left... then to the right... straight through the front door and into the street where he is hit by a lorry and killed. The bar falls silent. The father moans in grief. The barman cleans his glasses and whistles an old Irish tune. The father looks at the barman in disbelief and asks, "How can you be so cold and callous?" The barman says, "That boy should have quit while he was a head."

> **"If you want to offer encouragement in the delivery room, you might say things like, 'Hey, tremendous, you're really dilating beautifully.' To which she may well reply, 'F*** off. If it wasn't for you, I wouldn't be here.'"**
>
> *Jeremy Hardy*

A man phones up his local hospital and says, "Come quick! My wife's just gone into labour!" "I see," says the nurse answering the call. "And would this be her first child?" "No, you idiot!" says the man. "This is her husband!"

> **"For a father, a home birth is preferable. That way you're not missing anything on television."**
> **Jeremy Hardy**

At a prenatal class, the instructor gets the dads-to-be to each hold a bag of sand so they will have some idea of what it feels like to be pregnant. "This isn't so bad," says one of the men. "This doesn't weigh so much." "Right," says the instructor and drops a pen at his feet. "Now pick this pen up just like your wife would have to while she's pregnant." "OK" says the dad-to-be and turns to his wife, "Hey! Pick this pen up for me, will you?"

As Dad always says, "OK. So maybe we men can't ever experience the miracle of childbirth, but at least we can open all our own jars."

> **"I was born by Caesarean. You can't usually tell, but whenever I leave my house I go out by the window."**
> **Steven Wright**

A little boy was very much interested in the progress of his mother's pregnancy. Finally the day of the birth drew near and the boy overheard arrangements being made for his mother to go to the hospital. He looked at her puzzled and said, "Mum, I don't understand. If they're going to deliver the baby, why do you have to go to the hospital?"

Rather unusually it wasn't my mother but my father who died during childbirth. The idiot managed to get run over by the ambulance taking my mother to hospital.

Dad bumps into one of the new neighbours one morning and says, "I don't want to be rude, but you and your wife don't seem to have very much in common. What on earth possessed you to get married?" "It was that old thing of 'opposites attracting'," says the man. "I wasn't pregnant and she was."

> **"Poets have said that the reason to have children is to give yourself immortality. Immortality? Now that I have five children, my only hope is that they are all out of the house before I die."**
>
> **Bill Cosby**

A couple leave their gynaecologist's office with the wife in tears. They have just been told that the wife could never become pregnant and thus they will never be able to have the family they both desired so fervently. Suddenly, a masked man appears before them. "I think I can help you," he says, handing them a card. "Why are you masked?" the husband asks. "Because," says the mysterious masked man, "the government has declared my activities illegal. Go to the address on this card. The doctor will take a scraping from your mouth and culture it. In less than a year, we will have your baby for you." Turning to her husband, the wife exclaims, "This is the answer to our prayers!" Then she turns back to thank the stranger but finds him gone. "Just who was that masked man?" she asks her husband. "That," he answers, "was ... the Clone Arranger."

> **"It's not easy to juggle a pregnant wife and a troubled child, but somehow I manage to fit in eight hours of TV a day."**
>
> **Homer Simpson**

Parents-to-be are attending a prenatal class. The class is being taught all about the benefits of gentle exercise during pregnancy. "So," the instructor tells them, "a long slow walk is perfect exercise for you at this stage in the pregnancy. And if you want a bit of company then take your partner with you." "That's a great idea," says one of the dads, "but tell me, will my wife be able to carry a set of golf clubs in her condition?"

Three immigrants to the United Kingdom were just mastering the language. One was telling the others about the difficulty he was having in starting a family. He said, "I think my wife must be impregnable." The second said, "That's not the right word, she is inconceivable." To which the third replied, "You are both wrong, she is unbearable."

Things Expectant Fathers Should Know

Enjoy yourself while you still can.

Try to have twins – you don't want to go through this twice do you?

Have one last look at your bank statement – while it's still in credit.

Some idiot invented the baby pouch so that dads could carry the baby for nine months too – that must have been a woman.

Having children isn't a lifetime commitment – they'll be out of your hair in, ooh, 35 years max.

Get as much sleep as you can – you won't be getting much for the next couple of years.

Your wife won't be running up huge store card debts at

Debenhams any more – she'll be running them up at Mothercare instead.

Your wife may get sudden and bizarre cravings, such as lumps of coal and chocolate spread, but these will not be suitable gifts when you visit her in hospital.

If you attend the birth you may be shouted and sworn at quite a lot – still, you may as well start as she means to go on.

Babies do not have a volume control or an "off" switch.

Babies cannot be returned.

Everything your dad said to you will magically start coming out of your mouth as your children grow up.

You will be regularly given advice about child rearing by other people.

At least once a week you will hear the phrase "They don't come with an instruction manual do they?"

However cool you may think you are your children will increasingly see you as an embarrassment as they get older.

The reason children have so much energy is because they sap it out of their parents.

At the birth the gas and air is not intended for your use when you're getting a bit tired.

Mum will be shopping for two now.

Bad Reasons For Deciding To Have Children

To get those prime parking spaces near the supermarket door.

Because you think they will be less bother than a dog and slightly easier to train.

Because you think in their innocence they will look up to you and respect you as the greatest guy who ever lived.

Because you want an excuse to play with Scalextric again.

To enjoy cheaper travel with a Family Rail Card.

Because you've just thought up a really wacky name and need someone to bestow it upon.

Because Father's Day will give you one extra day a year when other people have to buy you stuff.

Because you need some extra people that you can bribe to support you in future arguments with Mum.

Because you think the Earth will greatly benefit if it's populated by more people just like you.

Because all your previous relationships with members of the human race have ultimately broken down, you've now decided you could have more success if you start from scratch and make your own people.

Because the more kids you have the more child benefit payments you'll get. Then maybe you'll be able to give up work altogether.

Because all your friends have got one.

You want someone to look after you when you're old.

Because you feel too embarrassed to go and watch kids' films by yourself.

You're a bit lonely.

Before And After Children

Before children	After children
Nights out were taken for granted	Nights out are taken before the babysitter changes her mind
Your money was your own	What money?
Family life seemed like a good idea	Doing a "Reggie Perrin" seems like a good idea
At weekends you got a lie-in	At weekends you have to lie to get out
Your parents used to ask you endless questions	Your kids ask you endless questions
You could go to bed as late as you liked	You go to bed as early as you can
You had parties and danced till dawn	You have parties and dance to the Teletubbies
You liked to think you were a bit of a sex machine	Your sex machine has become one of those gadgets that seemed like a good idea but which you now rarely use (a bit like a breadmaker)
You used to get embarrassed by the older generation	You are the older generation
You used to wander aimlessly around the house wondering what to do with yourself	Every time Mum or one of your kids sees you anywhere round the house, they provide you with a little job to do
You were desperately trying for a baby	You try desperately not to have any more babies
You enjoyed a life of pleasure	You seem to be enjoying a life at Her Majesty's pleasure

How Many?

A couple in Ireland have been trying for a baby for some time without success. In the end they ask a priest to pray for them. "I'll tell you what," says the priest. "I'll do better than that. I'm going to work in the Vatican for a while. While I'm there I'll go to the altar of Saint Peter and I'll light a candle for you." "Oh, bless you Father!" say the couple. Four years later the priest returns to Ireland and decides to call round and see how the couple are getting on. He finds a scene of mayhem. The woman is surrounded by 12 screaming children and is noticeably pregnant once again. "My goodness," says the priest. "What's happened?" "The first year," says the woman, "I had triplets. The second, I had quadruplets and last year quintuplets and now my husband has left me." "Oh my goodness," says the priest. "Where's he gone?" "He's gone to Rome, Father," says the woman. "To blow your bloody candle out."

Three men were discussing coincidences in a bar. The first man said, "My wife was reading *A Tale Of Two Cities* and she gave birth to twins." "That's funny," the second man remarked. "My wife was reading *The Three Musketeers* and she gave birth to triplets." "Bloody hell!" said the third man, "I've got to get home quickly." "Calm down" said the others, "what's the problem?" "Well," said the third man, "I've left my wife at home reading *Ali Baba and the Forty Thieves*."

A man whose wife was pregnant discovered he was a bit too squeamish to be in the delivery room at the time of the birth. So he had to ring up to see if the baby had arrived. He phoned the hospital and the nurse told him, "Congratulations! You've got a baby girl! But guess what! It looks like there's another one on the way!" The man had to ring back a little later and this time the nurse told him, "Your wife has just had another girl but guess what! There's another one coming!" The man had to ring back once more and the nurse told him, "Your wife has had a boy now but guess what! It looks like there's yet another one coming." The man couldn't stand any more of this so he went to the pub and had a few drinks. An hour later he decided he'd have to call the hospital again. When he dialled the number his hands were shaking so much he accidentally called a telephone sports line. So this time when he asked, "Hi! How many did we get in the end?" the person at the other end of the line told him, "It's 198 all out…. and the last one was a duck!"

Frequently Asked Questions For Parents To Be

Q: Can a mother get pregnant while breast-feeding?

A: Yes, but it's much easier if she removes the baby from her breast and puts him to sleep first.

Q: Does pregnancy affect a woman's memory?

A: Most of the ladies I asked don't remember.

Q: How will my wife know if the baby has dropped?

A: The baby will start crying. Tell your wife
to be more careful!

Q: Is there a reason I have to be in the delivery room
while my wife is in labour?

A: Not unless the word "alimony" is a concern for you.

Q: Is there a safe alternative to breast pumps?

A: Yes, baby lips.

Q: My midwife says it's not pain my partner will feel during
labour, but pressure. Is she right?

A: Yes, in the same way that a tornado might be
called an air current

Q: What are forceps?

A: Giant baby tweezers.

Q: What are night terrors?

A: Frightening episodes in which the new mother
dreams she's pregnant again.

Q: What causes baby blues?

A: Tanned, hard-bodied bimbos.

Q: What do you call a pregnancy that begins while
using birth control?

A: A misconception.

Q: What does it mean when a baby is born with teeth?

A: It means that the baby's mother may want to rethink her plans to breast-feed.

Q: What is colic?

A: A reminder for new parents to use birth control.

Q: What is the grasp reflex?

A: The reaction of a new father when he sees the new mother's breasts.

Q: What position should the baby be in during the ninth month of pregnancy?

A: Head down, pressing firmly on the mother's bladder.

Q: What's the best way to get a man to give up his seat to a pregnant woman?

A: Brute force.

Q: When does a woman's biological clock start ticking?

A: Right after she looks in the mirror and thinks, "Oh my God, crow's feet!"

Q: When should a baby not be circumcised?

A: When it's a girl.

Q: Will my partner love our dog less when the baby is born?

A: No, but you'll probably get on her nerves an awful lot.

Dad's Baby Name Dictionary

Barber's son: Harry
Birdwatcher's son: Robin
Bricklayer's son: Mason
Car mechanic's son: Jack
Carpenter's son: Woody
Cattle thief's son: Russell
Doctor's son: Bill
Entomologist's son: Nat
Ex-lion tamer's son: Claude
Exercise guru's son: Jim
Fence wire distributor's daughter: Barb
Fisherman's daughter: Annette
Fisherman's son: Rod
Gambler's daughter: Bette
Gambler's son: Chip
Hair stylist's son: Bob
Heredity expert's son: Gene
Homeopathic doctor's son: Herb
Hot-dog vendor's son: Frank
Ironworker's son: Rusty
Knight's son: Lance
Lawyer's daughter: Sue
Lawyer's son: Will
Lion tamer's son: Rory
Marksmanship instructor's daughter: Amy
Meteorologist's daughter: Haley
Mountaineer's son: Cliff
Movie star's son: Oscar
Oysterman's daughter: Shelley
Painter's son: Art
Sound stage technician's son: Mike
Steam shovel operator's son: Doug
Tailor's daughter: Jean
Thief's son: Rob
TV star's daughter: Emmy

Preparing For Fatherhood

See how long you can go without sleep then double it.

See how many synonyms you can find for "I'm knackered" – it will make your post-natal conversation a bit more sparkling.

Have one last look at your bank account while it's still in the black and perhaps frame it.

Look at a picture of your father and think, "This is what I'll look like in three years' time."

Say goodbye to your drinking friends.

Clean the inside of your car for the last time. It'll hardly be worth doing again in the next decade.

Practice sleeping standing up – this skill may be in surprisingly handy.

Start applying for jobs that will require extensive overseas travel or that will provide other prolonged periods away from home.

Look in the mirror and practise looking a bit frightening so you will have some chance of instilling a bit of discipline into your kids.

Give up trying to look frightening and practise bribing people with sweeties instead.

Go onto a GCSE revision website and start cramming for all the homework you're going to spend the next few years helping with.

Practise having conversations kneeling down. Not only will this prepare you for chatting to babies and small children, it will also prepare you for begging your wife to occasionally let you out of the house for the evening.

Set your alarm for one thirty a.m. (and three a.m., four a.m. and five thirty a.m.).

Buy a wet suit – essential for baby's bathtime and quite handy for mealtimes as well.

See if you can negotiate a bulk discount for buying a thousand nappies – you'll be surprised how quickly you get through them.

Things Dads Shouldn't Say To Mums When They're Pregnant

Can you not turn sideways when I'm trying to watch TV?

Are your ankles supposed to look like that?

I suppose now you've got to watch your alcohol intake I'll be drinking for two.

A bloke at work passed a stone the size of a pea. Wow, that must have hurt.

I know today's your due date, but Steve got a hole-in-one and that's a reason to celebrate, too, you know.

No really, I've always liked big women.

I've left the car keys are on the hall table. I'll see you at the hospital at half-time.

I was thinking that maybe we could name the baby after my secretary.

So this is what you're going to look like in 20 years' time!

No, I don't know where the remote control is! Have you looked under your breasts?

Not wishing to imply anything, but I don't think the baby can possibly weigh three stone.

Of course you'll get your figure back – we'll just search 1992 where you left it.

That's not a bun in the oven – it's the whole flipping bakery!

Was that a total eclipse or did you just walk past the window?

Now why on earth would I want to rub your feet?

You know, looking at her, you'd never guess that Jordan has had a baby!

You know, now that you mention it, you are getting fat and unattractive.

Perhaps I should sleep in the spare room for the last few weeks in case you roll on top of me in the night?

Looking at the size of you, love, I'd say it must be twins – at least.

A couple of tent poles and I reckon I could knock up a gazebo out of your maternity dress when you've finished with it.

This maternity leave lark's a bit of a con really, isn't it? If you were in China you'd be working in a paddy field right up to the last minute.

I tell you, if men had babies they wouldn't make half the fuss you women make.

Let's just pray the baby doesn't come early and clash with the World Cup Final – it'd be a shame to miss the birth of my own child.

I know women have obsessive cravings when they're pregnant, but your chocolate one has been going on for over 30 years now.

Why do I have to come to antenatal classes? You're the one having the baby.

I want the night of the birth to be special so I've bought myself a bottle of single malt and an expensive cigar.

Dads And Babies

When mum hears a noise downstairs in the middle of the night it's dad who goes to investigate because dads aren't scared of burglars. When a big hairy spider (or even a small, bald spider) needs removing from the bath it's dad who does it because dads aren't scared of spiders, but when it comes to babies – dads are terrified!

They're so small! What if I drop it? What am I supposed to do with it? What if it starts crying? What if it stops breathing? Which end does the food go in again? As far as dad's concerned there's a good reason why it's women that have babies. Now if they had wheels, or you could plug them in or take them to bits when they went wrong, then you'd be talking, but they're just so, well, a bit girly really – even the boys. You have to dress them and feed them and put them to bed – why can't women just have dolls? But no, they want babies. Real ones. Ones that chew everything – apart from the food you try and put in their mouths; ones that need their nappies changing about every five minutes – especially when mum's "just popped out"; and ones who wake up at hours you never even knew existed.

But they're not babies forever. Only 'til your hair is turning grey, your nerves are in shreds and your bank balance is in the red. No, they grow out of all those childish habits like drawing on the walls, eating soil from the garden or being sick down your back and eventually life gets back to something approaching normality. Then your wife has a great idea: "Darling, wouldn't it be nice to have another one?" Aarrghh!

"I must confess, I was born at a very early age."

Groucho Marx

A professional rugby player is walking down the street one day when he passes a block of flats with smoke pouring out of the upper storey windows. A woman with a baby in her arms is shouting down to him from the fifth floor. "Help! I can't get down!" she cries. "The lift's broken and there's smoke billowing up the stairwell." "OK," says the rugby player. "Don't panic. I'll help you. I'm a professional rugby player. So throw your baby down and I promise you I'll catch him." "That's impossible," says the mum. "No," says the rugby player. "Trust me. I've never missed a catch in my career." So the woman aims carefully and throws her baby down. The rugby player, true to his word, braces himself, stands with his legs apart and catches the baby in his hands like a rugby ball. The woman breathes an immense sigh of relief but then, somewhat unfortunately, the rugby player gets carried away, bounces the baby three times and kicks him back over the top of the building for a conversion.

> **"To be a successful father, there's one absolute rule: when you have a kid, don't look at it for the first two years."**
> **Ernest Hemingway**

A new dad was having a go at trying to feed his first baby with some strained peas. Mum walked in and found traces of the food all over the kitchen. She looked round at the walls and then at the dad sitting next to the baby, staring into space. "What the hell do you think you're doing?" she asked. "Don't worry," said Dad, "I'm just waiting for the first coat to dry then I'll give him some more."

A worried father says to his wife, "I see the baby's nose is running again." "Oh honestly!" she snaps back. "Can't you think of anything except the horse racing?"

When he was born they could tell little Timmy was going to be a bit of a criminal. "Oh look," they said. "He's got his mother's eyes and his father's nose. And look, now he's got the midwife's purse."

> **"Getting down on all fours and imitating a rhinoceros stops babies from crying. (Put an empty cigarette pack on your nose for a horn and make loud 'snort' noises). I don't know why parents don't do this more often. Usually it makes the kid laugh. Sometimes it sends him into shock. Either way it quiets him down. If you're a parent, acting like a rhino has another advantage. Keep it up until the kid is a teenager and he definitely won't have his friends hanging around your house all the time."**
> **P J O'Rourke**

TRUE STORY

A couple were having trouble getting their three-year-old son potty-trained. One day the father took him and his baby sister out to the park and then to a cafe for a snack. When the food arrived Dad smelt a familiar smell. "Oh no," he thought. "Why does the baby have to fill her nappy now?" So he had a discreet peek and she was clean. He then realized it must have been his son who had had an "accident" so he asked him, "David, have you messed yourself?" "No, Dad, I just 'popped'." "Are you sure, David?" asked the father, with the smell now getting strong enough to gain disapproving glances from other people eating their meals nearby. "Just wind is it?" asked Dad. "Yes, Dad. If you don't believe me..." And with that he pulled his trousers and pants down, bent over and offered his backside for inspection in full view of the entire restaurant.

One night a wife found her husband standing staring intently at their sleeping baby's cot. She watched him for a few moments as he stood looking down at the infant and saw on his face a mixture of emotions: disbelief, doubt, delight, amazement, enchantment and scepticism. She was touched by this unusual display on her husband's part and with her eyes glistening, she slipped her arms around him and asked, "A penny for your thoughts?" "I just can't believe it," said the dad. "It's completely amazing to me!" "I know," says the mum. "Isn't our baby beautiful?" "No," says the dad. "It's the cot. I just can't see how anyone could manufacture one like this and manage to sell it for only £46.50."

A woman is having a baby. In the delivery room the father asks the nurses if there is anything he can do to help. The nurse replies, "No. Please wait outside." After five minutes, he asks the same question and gets the same reply. This carries on until the baby is born when, once again, the father asks if there is anything he can do. This time the nurse says, "OK. If you want, you can wash the baby." The father is thrilled and goes off to perform his task. After a while, the nurse returns to check on the baby and finds the father with his fingers in the baby's nostrils moving it around in the water as if it was a boat. "What are you doing?" exclaims the nurse. "That's not the way you wash a baby." The father replies, "It is when the water's too hot!"

Things Dad Shouldn't Be Doing On Paternity Leave

Getting away for a few days on his own.

Expecting tea in bed in the morning.

Seeing if the baby seat can be fitted into the golf buggy.

Chatting up other mums at the clinic.

Using it as a golden opportunity to do some job hunting.

Inviting his unemployed mates round for afternoon drinking sessions.

Starting his own blog about how tough it is being a dad.

Offering to look after the baby while the wife gets on with some decorating.

Enjoying himself.

Taking up smoking again.

Wishing he were back at work.

Having afternoon naps.

Finding time to start a new hobby.

Denying that the baby's his.

Still trying to assemble the flat pack cot.

The Instructions A Father Should Get With A New Baby

Warning: this is not a toy.

Does not require batteries. Though is still capable of functioning for many hours at a time.

Product can be maintained by regular input of food solids into upper aperture.

In the early stages it may appear that the major proportion of food solids are not remaining in the upper aperture; but with perseverance it should be possible to successfully deposit at least 30 per cent, which will be sufficient for product maintenance.

If food solids reappear from lower aperture almost immediately do not contact customer helpline – this is normal.

Lower aperture may also emit odd odours and noises – this too is normal.

Product will need constant attention in order to maintain optimum performance, but with correct handling may be capable of independent maintenance after a certain period – anywhere between 18 and 40 years.

This product also contains an in-built alarm facility. Unfortunately, due to a design fault, it is not possible to programme the exact time at which you wish to be awakened.

The alarm facility also contains a "snooze" function which can be operated by:

a. Attaching product to wife
b. Gentle rocking of product (also see "voice recognition function" below)

Voice recognition function: this sophisticated state-of-the-art product also contains a voice recognition system. If you require the product to go into sleep mode simply sing the words, "twinkle twinkle little star, how I wonder what you are," over and over whilst gently rocking the product for anything up to an hour. If this fails, or when arms are tired, try option "a" above.

The product also contains a rudimentary speech function. In the early stages of ownership this will consist of what appear to be meaningless gurgles and babbling. The discerning user, however, will soon be able to group these seemingly meaningless mutterings into the following broad categories:

I'm hungry
I'm grumpy
I'm hungry and grumpy
I'm grumpy because I'm hungry
I'm blaming you for any or all of the above

The voice recognition system will, in time, be capable of replicating the language of the user. Unfortunately, due to another design fault the product will lose the ability to replicate human speech after approximately 13 years.

Please note:
Product must not be dropped, left unattended or re-sold. This product does not come with a warranty, and whilst expected to give many hours of pleasure this cannot be guaranteed.

Note: product cannot be returned to manufacturer under any circumstances.

Essential Requirements Of Being A Dad

To be good enough at football that your children will be impressed, but not so good that they think you're showing off.

To be able to make up bedtime stories that are so long and dull that your children will be asleep in minutes.

To be able to drive quite happily and completely ignore a full-scale punch-up going on in the back of the car.

To be able to read the whole paper in one sitting on the toilet, because you know it's the only chance you'll get.

To be able to change a nappy with one hand and operate the TV remote control with the other.

To possess a ready supply of fully charged batteries ready for whatever toy or household gadget conks out next.

To be possessed of lightning quick reflexes so you can click and close any dodgy websites that pop up accidentally on the computer during the course of researching "homework".

To have enough strength to pick up and spin small children in the air for sufficient time to make them feel quite sick, but not quite enough strength to carry on until they actually are.

To have no qualms about hogging the TV remote control all evening.

To have your own personal chair in the living room that the kids aren't allowed to sit on and which you therefore presume will be commonly referred to as "Dad's throne".

To possess a secret stash of Superglue strong enough to fix anything in the house that happens to fall apart – including the kid.

To have apparently intense interest in some hobby or pastime and a special room, shed or workshop in which this may be privately pursued, even if it's just an excuse to escape the rest of the family occasionally. NB: these must be proper Dad-style interests such as fashioning pipe racks and constructing models of the Flying Scotsman out of matchsticks. Porn does not count!

Signs You Are A New Dad

A one-hour break from the baby is a vast expanse of time into which you can fit 1001 things.

All your friends are dads too.

Changing a nappy is still a charming novelty.

Getting four hours of consecutive sleep is a privilege.

Getting six hours of sleep is a privilege.

The bags under your eyes have been replaced with entire luggage sets.

The list of bodily fluids that disgust you has shortened, possibly to zero.

The sentence, "Darling, could you take his foot out of my pocket?" sounds normal.

The thought of your mother-in-law coming over for a few hours is a pleasant one.

When the milkman calls at five thirty a.m. you're already up.

You answer the question "How are you?" with "We're fine."

You are used to doing everything one-handed.

You can assemble a baby buggy in a rainstorm in ten seconds flat.

The decision as to whether or not a shirt is wearable is based not on sweatiness, but upon how well the baby sick stains match the shirt's main colour.

You feel acute anxiety if you're left on your own with the baby for more than 20 minutes.

You find yourself whistling nursery rhymes.

You go to bed at nine-thirty just to be sure of a bit of sleep.

You panic every time the baby cries – and every time it doesn't.

You see a slender teenage girl walking down your street, and you think, "Hey, I wonder if I could interest her in... babysitting?"

Your idea of romance is holding hands.

You're already planning the train set, remote control cars and computer games you're going to buy.

You've given up cleaning the inside of the car.

But Can Dad Be Sure It's His?

A man is very proud to have six children and on every possible occasion he announces the fact to the world. One of his ruses is to loudly refer to his wife as "Mother of Six" whenever they're in a crowded place together. After a while his wife gets increasingly fed up with this amusing nickname. Finally at a big party he calls through the crowd, "OK, Mother of Six? Are you ready to go home now?" and she replies, "Certainly am, Father of Four."

A man arrives back after a long business trip to find his son is playing with an expensive new X–Box. "Hey! How did you get that?" asks Dad. "I bought it," says the little boy. "Bought it?" says Dad. "How did you get the money for that?" "I earned it," says the boy. "Hiking." "Hiking!" says Dad. "Who gets paid for going hiking?" "I do," replies the boy. "Every time Uncle Bob came round to see Mummy while you were away, he gave me 20 pounds and then told me to take a hike."

> **"The other night I told my kid, 'Someday, you'll have children of your own.' He said, 'So will you.'"**
>
> **Rodney Dangerfield**

After years in rented accommodation a couple finally save up enough money to buy their own house. One of their old flatmates helps them with the move and while they're not looking he hides a surprise housewarming present of a bottle of champagne in a cupboard. Unfortunately the bottle gets shoved to the back of the cupboard and doesn't turn up for several years. They finally find it just in time to toast the arrival of their third baby. Mum pours out the champagne for all of their friends and family who have come round to "wet the baby's head" while Dad proudly reads out the message that their old friend has written on the label: "Make sure you take care of this one because, this time, it's actually yours!"

At school, one of the older boys teaches little Johnny a good trick. "All grown-ups have a secret," says the older boy. "You just have to pretend you know what it is and then they'll get you anything you want." So Johnny decides to try this out when he gets home and, in a very serious voice, says to his mum, "Mum, I know the whole truth." His mother becomes flustered. She tells him, "OK. Just whatever you do, don't tell your father." And then she hands him 20 pounds. "Wow," thinks Johnny. "This is going well." So next he waits for his dad to get home from work. When Dad arrives Johnny greets him in the hallway, looking very solemn and serious and tells him, "Dad! I know the whole truth." "Oh my goodness," says Dad and gives him 40 pounds. "Well, whatever you do, don't say a word to your mother." "Fantastic," thinks Johnny and decides to play the trick again on the next adult who comes to the door. The next morning the doorbell rings and there on the front doorstep is the milkman. Little Johnny stands and looks at the milkman very solemnly before telling him, "I know the whole truth." "Really?" says the milkman looking surprised. Then he smiles broadly, throws opens his arms and says, "Well, come on then! Give your daddy a hug!"

A Chinese dad is really worried after he and his wife have their first baby. He runs round to the doctor's to ask for some medical advice. "Doctor," he says. "I'm sure the new baby isn't mine. He's been born with red hair. Look at me! My hair's completely black and so is my wife's. The baby can't be mine!" "Don't be silly," says the doctor. "It doesn't matter that you and your wife have both got black hair. Maybe one of your grandparents or great-grandparents had red hair." "No," says the dad. "It's simply not possible. Both my wife and myself are from pure Asian ancestry. There has never been anyone in either of our families who has red hair." "OK," says the doctor. "But there's got to be some other reason for it. Tell me, how often do you and your wife have sex?" "Well," says the dad, "I'm a very busy man so we don't often get the chance. In fact recently I've been working so hard I think we've only made love twice in the last 16 months." "Ah ha!" says the doctor. "There's your explanation. It's rust!"

One day a young polar bear was sitting on an ice floe, watching his father catching fish through a hole in the ice. All of a sudden he asked, "Daddy, am I a real polar bear?" His father said, "Of course you're a real polar bear." Then the young bear asked, "Are you absolutely sure that I'm 100 per cent polar bear, Dad?" "Of course you are, son," said Dad. "I'm a polar bear, your mum's a polar bear, the whole family are polar bears..." "But, Dad," said the little polar bear. "Are you sure there's not a little bit of brown bear in me?" "No, son. Absolutely not." "Are you really, really sure, Dad, that there's not maybe just a little bit of black bear in me?" "No, son, not even a little bit." "Maybe just a little bit of grizzly bear, Dad?" "Oh for goodness sake!" said the exasperated father bear. "No! No! No! Why are you asking all these questions?" The little polar bear replied, "Because, Dad, I'm flipping well freezing my backside off out here!"

Names For The Baby That Dad Will Suggest

The Christian names of all of the current squad of his favourite football team

Dad will have no qualms about this despite the fact that every time you call them by their full name, it will sound like you are doing the roll call for an Italian primary school class or perhaps announcing the firemen in the Latin American version of *Trumpton*.

Funny initials

Watch out for this one, mum! Dad may well suggest an apparently ordinary set of names that is ultimately designed to provide his offspring with hilarious initials, e.g. Barney Oliver Green, Stephen Henry Ignatius Thompson, Freddie Andrew Robert Timothy Young etc. If dad's subtle humour is not immediately noticed and appreciated, don't worry, it'll get plenty of attention as soon as the poor kid starts school!

Aaron

As comedian Michael McIntyre has noted, this is the worst name you can possibly give a child. The reason: it's the very first name in the *Baby Name Book*! By choosing this one you will make yourselves look like the laziest parents in the entire world.

The name of his hero

Sometimes this will work. Sometimes it won't. Sometimes it may give mum pause for thought as regards certain aspects of dad's personality. For example, if dad suggests Winston for his son's name, that might be OK. Adolf, on the other hand, has not come back into fashion at the time of writing. Similarly, if dad seriously suggests naming the little one Osama, Manson, Lucifer, Davros Dark Lord of the Daleks or George W, it might be time for mum to reconsider whether he's going to make an entirely suitable father figure.

His own dad's name

This could be a nice idea but mum should make sure that dad fully understands the concept and doesn't attempt to have his son and heir baptized with the name "Granddad".

Wacky names

Stig, Tiger, Toto etc may all be quite cool, but if dad tries to name the child Fifi Trixibelle this may again indicate aspects of his personality that have to date remained hidden from the world. Particularly if he attempts to give this name to his son.

An ultra macho name

Some dads may opt to give their sons macho names such as Hunter, Rocky, Clint, Duke, Randy Savage The Third etc. Dads might be tempted to do this particularly if their own fathers bestowed names which were (arguably) from the opposite end of the macho spectrum upon them, e.g. Timothy, Quentin, Tarquin, Algernon, Fifi Trixibelle etc.

His own name

Lots of people do this, but they are extremely arrogant, incredibly lazy or labouring under the misapprehension that they have in fact produced a cloned copy of themselves. It will also, of course, result in future confusion around the house with Mum saying things like, "Warren! It's time for you to get off to work! Warren! It's time for you to go to school! Oh look at you, Warren! You've got something sticky in your hair, you've managed to get your breakfast all down your front and I do believe you've also wet your pants! No, not you, Warren, I'm talking to your father." The boxer George Foreman, on the other hand, had no problem with naming his five sons George (George Jr, George III, George IV and George V). His daughters, however, are named Michi, Freeda, Georgetta, Natalie and Leola. Even though he doesn't seem to have realized that there were female forms of the name George until he reached daughter number three, you've got to hand it to him for avoiding the more obvious Georgia or Georgina.

Genuine Extracts From Letters Applying For Welfare

Both sides of my parents is very poor and I can't expect anything from them as my mother has been in bed for one year with one doctor and she won't take another.

Do I get more than I am getting?

I am a poor woman and all I have is gone.

I am forwarding my marriage certificate and six children. I had seven, but one died which was baptized on a half sheet of paper.

I am forwarding my marriage certificate and my three children, one of which is a mistake as you can see.

I am glad to say my husband who has been missing is now deceased.

I am very much annoyed to find that you have branded my son illiterate. This is a dirty lie, as I was married to his father a week before he was born.

I am writing the welfare department to say that my baby was born two years old. When do I get my money?

I cannot get sick pay, I got six children, can you tell me why this is?

I have no children as yet, as my husband is a truck driver and works day and night.

I have two children and my husband cannot supply enough milk.

I want money as quick as I can get it. I have been in bed with the doctor for two weeks and he doesn't do me any good. If things don't improve, I will have to send for another doctor.

In accordance with your instructions I have given birth to a boy that weighs 101 pounds. I hope this is satisfactory.

In accordance with your instructions I have given birth to twins in the enclosed envelope.

Mrs Jones has not had any clothes for two years and has been visited regularly by the clergy.

My husband got his project cut off about two weeks ago and I haven't had any relief since.

My husband has worked about one shift two months ago and now he has left me, and I ain't had no pay since he has gone, nor before either.

Please find for certain if my husband is dead. The man I am now living with can't do anything until he knows.

Please send me a letter and tell me if my husband has made applications for a wife and child.

Please send me my elopement as I have a four months old baby and he is my only support and I kneed all I get every day to buy food and keep in close.

This is my eighth child. What are you going to do about it?

Unless I get my husband's money pretty soon, I will be forced to lead an immortal life.

You have changed my little boy to a girl. Will this make any difference?

Mums And Dads

The good cop/bad cop of the parenting world. When mums face difficult parenting decisions, such as whether a child is allowed to have an expensive new computer, have their ears pierced for the first time or have a third doughnut, they say, "ask your father". When dad says "no" then he's the bad guy. After a while most dads learn the useful response, "ask your mother".

Then there's the question of discipline. Somehow the threat of "wait 'til your father gets home" is nearly always worse than the reality. By the time Dad does get home either everyone's forgotten what the problem was in the first place or he's too tired to work up his role as Terminator in carpet slippers.

But the roles are still quite well defined. Despite women's lib, new men, and all the rest of it, mum is usually good cop and dad is usually bad cop. One of the kids has crashed their bike and grazed their knees? It's dad who has to go and buy a new wheel so don't expect any sympathy from him. Mum says "How awful!" and gets out a tissue. Dad says "How much?" and gets out his wallet.

And nine times out of ten it's dad who makes sure he's at work all day while mum has to be around for all those full-on parenting duties, such as school runs, doctor's appointments, clothes buying, etc. But there are some things dad can do that mum can't: turn children upside down for no good reason, actually enjoy playing computer games and football, and feed their kids on junk food all weekend without feeling the slightest bit guilty.

Mums and dads – they're a team!

Dr. Hugo Hackenbush (Groucho Marx): (Pointing to a portrait of one of Judy's parents) You know, I proposed to your mother once.
Judy: But that's my father!
Dr. Hugo Hackenbush: No wonder he turned me down.

The Marx Brothers—A Day At The Races

Mum, of course, knows everything about her children. Mum knows about best friends, best and worst subjects at school, biggest fears, what they want for Christmas, their ambitions, hopes and dreams in life, not to mention their favourite dinners and when they're due at the dentist. Dad, on the other hand, is vaguely aware that there are some small people who live in his house with him.

One day dad's youngest little boy says to him, "Dad, I've decided I want to get married." "Oh yes," says Dad. "And who are you going to get married to?" "Grandma," says the little boy. "What?" says Dad. "Don't you think it's going to be a problem if you marry my mother." "I don't see why," says the little boy. "You married mine."

A little boy asks, "Dad, why do you and Mum argue all the time?" "I don't know, son," says Dad. "She never tells me."

TRUE STORY

An eight-year-old girl was asked what she thought her mum and dad had in common with each other. She answered, "Both of them don't want any more kids."

A little girl and a little boy were at nursery one day. The girl approaches the boy and says, "Hey Tommy, do you want to play 'Mummies and Daddies?" He says, "OK. What do you want me to do?" The girl replies, "I want you to communicate your thoughts." "Communicate my thoughts?" says a bewildered Tommy, "I have no idea what that means." The little girl smirks and says, "Perfect. You can be the husband."

A man tells a friend one night, "Personally, I think one of the greatest things about marriage is that as both husband and father, I can say anything I want to around the house. Of course, no one pays the slightest bit of attention."

As dad will never fail to point out, the number one cause of divorce is marriage.

Dad says he can remember where he got married, he can remember when he got married, he can even remember to whom he got married. He just can't remember why.

If it wasn't for the institution of marriage, dads could sail happily through their whole lives not realising that they had any faults at all.

Dad says to a friend, "You know I've been happily married for ten years." "I thought you got married 25 years ago," says his friend. "That's right," says Dad. "And ten out of 25 isn't too bad, is it?"

A woman marries a man expecting he will change, but he doesn't. A man marries a woman expecting she won't change, but she does.

Q: What's the difference between a girlfriend and a wife?
A: About four stone.

Dad says, "Love may be blind but marriage is a real eye-opener."

Dad tells his kids, "A happy marriage is based on giving and taking. I give and your mother takes."

Did you hear about the man who had the following inscription on his tombstone: "I never knew what real happiness was until I got married; then it was too late."

Dad and Mum's marriage has gone through many stages. For the first couple of years, Dad did all the talking and Mum listened. For the next few years, Mum did all the talking and Dad listened. After that they've both been the ones talking and the neighbours have been the ones listening.

As Dad always says, "If love is blind and marriage is an institution, then this must mean that marriage is an institution for the blind."

And as Dad then usually goes on to say, "Marriage is a thing that takes just a few short minutes to get into, but a lifetime to get out of."

And then he adds, "Man is incomplete until he gets married. After that he is finished."

Before following it up with, "My marriage was made in heaven; but so are thunder and lightning."

Dad says he's come to a few conclusions about marriage. He says it's a bit like going to a posh restaurant. You spend a very long time deciding what you want, but as soon as you get it, you wish you'd ordered what the person on the next table has got instead.

Mum tells her daughter, "If it's true that girls tend to marry men like their fathers, that probably explains why mothers always cry at weddings."

Dad claims after many years he's come to a conclusion about marriage. He says it's an incredibly expensive way to get your laundry done for nothing.

Dad says he hasn't looked at another woman since the day he got married. He says Mum has put him off for life.

Q: Do married men live longer than single men?
A: No. It just seems longer.

A man once placed an advert in the back of a newspaper. It simply read, "Wife wanted." The day it appeared he was inundated with messages all saying the same thing: "You can have mine."

Marriage is the triumph of imagination over intelligence. Second marriage is the triumph of hope over experience.

Mum and Dad are having a huge row. Eventually Mum shouts, "If you say one more word, I promise you I am going straight home to Mother!" Dad pauses for a moment, then opens the window, leans out and calls, "Taxi!!"

TRUE STORY

One day a mum found her five-year-old boy sitting in his bedroom looking quite worried. "What's the matter?" she asked him. "I don't know what will happen with this bed when I get married," said the boy. "How will my wife fit in?"

Dad was in his usual place sitting at the table, reading the paper after breakfast. He came across an article about a beautiful actress who was about to marry a football player who was well known for his low IQ and lack of general knowledge. He turned to his wife with a look of disbelief on his face. "I'll never understand why the biggest idiots in this world get the most attractive wives." His wife replied, "Why thank you, dear!"

One evening Dad comes home from work, falls in a heap on the sofa in front of the TV and calls out to Mum, "Get me a drink before it starts." So Mum goes to the fridge and gets him a cold beer. Ten minutes later he's gulped it down and calls out, "Get me another drink before it starts." She fumes inwardly, but gets another beer anyway. Ten minutes later he says, "Get me another drink, I think it's going to start any time now." By this time Mum is hopping mad. She shouts, "Is that all you're going to do all night? Sit in front of the TV and knock back beer? Why, you're just a lazy, booze-swilling slob, and what's more..." At this point Dad rolls his eyes heavenwards, sighs and says, "Oh no! It's started!"

Mum tells Dad one day, "Before we got married, you told me you were quite well off." "I was," says Dad. "Unfortunately at the time I didn't realize quite how much."

Mum and Dad have been having an argument. "You know what?" says Mum. "I must have been a fool when I agreed to marry you." "I know," says Dad. "But at the time I was in love so I didn't notice."

Smart man + Smart Woman = Romance
Smart Man + Dumb Woman = Pregnancy
Dumb Man + Smart Woman = Affair
Dumb Man + Dumb Woman = Marriage

One day Dad decides that things have got to a critical point in his marriage and he phones an agony aunt on the radio. "If things are really that bad," she tells him, "you should face up to reality, be honest about it and leave your wife." "Well," says Dad, "I would, if only I could think of a way of doing it that wouldn't make her happy."

One day Mum finds Dad studying their marriage certificate very carefully. After a while Mum asks him, "Are you looking for something there? "Yes," replies Dad. "The expiration date."

> **"My marriage was my dad's idea. She was the girl next door and her father had an electric drill."**
>
> **Ronnie Corbett**

Dad runs into the house one night and yells to Mum, "Right, pack up your things! I've just won the Lottery!" Mum shouts back, "Shall I pack for warm weather or cold?" Dad replies, "I don't care, just as long as you're out of the house by midnight!"

One day Dad looks at Mum and says, "Your chest is quite flat now isn't it? And are your legs are quite hairy. Do you ever get mistaken for a man?" "No," says Mum. "Do you?"

When Mum and Dad got married they agreed never to go to bed angry with each another. They're currently the world record holders having been awake for 18 years!

Dad says to Mum one night, "OK! Get your coat! I'm going out to the pub!" "Oh good," says Mum. "So you're taking me with you are you?" "No," says Dad. "I'm leaving you here and switching the heating off."

> **Barbara: It's unlucky to see the bride on the morning of the wedding.**
> **Jim: I don't remember seeing you that morning.**
> *The Royle Family*

Dad walks into a pub one night after work and orders a double scotch. He knocks it back, looks inside his jacket pocket and then orders another double scotch. When he's finished it, he looks inside his pocket again and asks for yet another double scotch. The barmaid, who can't contain her curiosity any longer asks, "I don't want to be nosy, but how come you look inside your jacket pocket each time just before you order a drink?" Dad says, "I'm looking at a picture of my missus. When she starts to look attractive, I know it's time to go home."

Two dads are talking. "My wife's an angel," says the first. "You lucky old so and so," says the second. "Mine's still alive."

A little boy says to his dad, "Is it true, Dad, that in some parts of Africa a man doesn't know his wife until he marries her?" Dad replies, "That's the way it is in every country, son."

In a small town in the Midlands, there was quite a large factory that hired only married men. Concerned about this, a local

feminist newspaper reporter called on the owner and asked
him, "Why is it you limit your employees to married men? Is it
because you think women are weak, stupid, lazy... or what?"
"No, not at all, Madam," the manager said. "It's because our
employees are used to obeying orders, are accustomed to being
shoved around, know when to keep their mouths shut and
don't sulk when I shout at them."

Advice From Kids

When your mum is mad at your dad, don't let her brush your
hair.

Eleven-year-old girl

One day Mum comes home to find the house has been burgled
and the whole place in total upheaval: cupboard doors swinging
open, drawers pulled out, clothes strewn all over the place,
but she doesn't call the police until the following day. When a
policeman comes to take the details he asks why she left it so
long before reporting it. "Well officer," she replies, "I wasn't
sure at first whether we had been burgled or whether it had just
been my husband searching for a clean shirt."

Things are quite bad at the moment for Dad and he's been
extremely depressed. He says Mum has threatened to walk out
on him... but even that hasn't cheered him up.

Top tip for dads with jealous wives: if you really want to drive
her crazy don't talk in your sleep, just smile contentedly.

A young mother dials 999 and asks for the police, "I want
to report the man next door," says the woman. "He's forever
spying on me." "What makes you think that, Madam?" asks the
police operator. "Well," says the young mum, "every time I peep
through the window into his house, he's peeping back at me."

A newspaper recently published the findings of a new survey about marital relationships. According to the study, married men's top fantasy during sex is to imagine their wives aren't fantasizing.

A woman went to the police station with her next-door neighbour to report that her husband was missing. The policeman asked for a description. She said, "He's 35 years old, six foot four, has the most beautiful blue eyes, dark wavy hair, an athletic build, is soft-spoken and is good to the children." The next-door neighbour protested, "Your husband is five foot four, chubby, bald, has a big mouth and is nasty to your children." The wife replied, "Yes, but who wants HIM back?"

> **"I got a letter from my mother… 'Since you left home your father has become a sex maniac and tries to make love to me every opportunity he gets. Please excuse the wobbly writing.'"**
> **Frank Carson**

A couple and their ten-year-old son live in a high-rise flat in the middle of town, but because it's small there's not much privacy, so the couple decide that the only way they can have a Sunday afternoon quickie is to send their son out onto the balcony and ask him to report on what he can see outside. The couple go to bed and the boy begins his observations, "There's a car being clamped across the road," he begins. "I can see a police car and a fire engine up the road, and Mr Jones is taking his dog for a walk." After a short silence he says, "There's a delivery at the supermarket and the Thompsons are having sex." Mum and Dad sit up suddenly in bed. "How do you know the Thompsons are having sex?" says Dad incredulously. The boy says matter-of-factly, "Because their little girl is standing out on the balcony as well."

Two young men are in the pub talking about their problems. "My girlfriend and I want to get married," says the first. "But I don't know how we can afford anywhere to live." "Can't you move in and live with your girlfriend's parents?" asks his friend. "Not really," says the first man. "They're still living with their parents."

Dad's little boy is watching, fascinated, as his mother smoothes cold cream all over her face. "Why do you do that, Mummy?" he asks. "To make myself beautiful," says his mum and then begins dabbing the cream off with a tissue. "What's the matter?" asks the boy. "Giving up now?"

Mum and Dad are talking. "Do you think our son got his brains from me?" says Mum. "Probably," says Dad. "I've still got mine."

Dad went to the dentist and said, "How much will it cost to have three teeth taken out?" "£150" said the dentist. "That's ridiculous," said Dad. "Well," said the dentist, "I could cut down the anaesthetic and it would cost £80." "That's still too expensive," said Dad. "OK, if I don't use any anaesthesia I could knock the price down to £20," said the dentist. "Still too much," said Dad." Well one of my students can do it for £10," said the dentist. "Perfect," said Dad. "Book my missus in for next Tuesday".

"Happiness is having a large, loving, caring close-knit family – in another city."
George Burns

My relatives are in the iron and steel business. My mother irons and my father steals.

Two dads are talking. One says to the other, "So, you say you managed to win that argument with your wife the other day?" "Oh yes," says the second dad. "She came crawling to me on her hands and knees." "Honestly?" asks the first. "What did she say?" "She said, 'Are you going come out from under that bed, you coward?'"

Dad says Mum always knows exactly what he needs to buy her for the house next... almost immediately after the neighbours get one.

TRUE STORY

Mum and her oldest son arrived back at home late one night. Mum was annoyed to find that she had gone out without her keys and so was now locked out. The pair tried knocking on the door and then on the windows to get someone to come and let them in. Mum knew Dad and her younger son and daughter were in the house, but they all seemed to be fast asleep, because after several minutes no one had come to the door. Mum tried sounding the car horn, which woke up the neighbours, but still failed to rouse anyone in their own house. In the end Mum had to call the home phone and woke her younger son. He came down and let them in. Inside they found Dad snoring away in front of the television. Mum quietly switched the set off at which point Dad immediately sat bolt upright and shouted, "Hey! What are you doing? I was just watching that!"

It's sad how whole families are sometimes torn apart by simple things, like wild dogs.

Two dads are talking one day when one observes to the other, "Of course if a word begins with 'tele' it must have something to do with communication. All the fastest forms of communication start with 'tele'." "And what are they?" asks his friend. "Telephone, Television and Tell–a–woman."

A man is a person who, if a woman says to him, "Never mind, I'll do it myself," lets her. A woman is a person who, if she says to a man, "Never mind, I'll do it myself," and he lets her, gets annoyed. A man is a person who, if a woman says to him, "Never mind, I'll do it myself," and he lets her and she gets annoyed, asks, "Now what are you annoyed about?" A woman is a person who, if she says to a man, "Never mind, I'll do it myself," and he lets her, and she gets annoyed, and he says, "Now what are you annoyed about?" tells him, "Well, if you don't know, I'm not going to tell you!"

Dad says that if you hear your dog barking at your back door and your wife knocking on your front door, it is the dog that you should go to first, because there's a chance that he will shut up once he gets in.

Mum tells Dad one day, "It's a well known fact that a woman's mind is cleaner than a man's." "Well, you know why that is," says Dad. "She changes it more often."

Dads' Multiple Choice Quiz

Are you a fun dad? You probably think you're a fun dad. You unfailingly put on a party hat at Christmas dinner, you make corny jokes that only your family could love, and you have hair growing out of amusing places such as your nose and ears. What kid wouldn't love a dad like that? Well, sorry to break the news to you, but kids these days want a bit more of an all-rounder. A sort of cross between a Chuckle brother, James Bond and David Beckham. Tough call, yes, but try the following quiz and see how you shape up.

The kids want to play football, do you:

a) Take them to the nearest park and let them have a good old kick around, and perhaps let the odd ball in when it's your turn to be goalie?

b) Take them to the park and spend two hours running rings round them with your dribbling and goal scoring skills, and bring them home exhausted?

c) Reluctantly dig out your dusty old Subbuteo set and let them play with it while you carry on reading the paper?

One of your younger children wants a birthday party with lots of friends, do you:

a) Help mum cart home a bootload of goodies from the supermarket, blow up balloons, decorate the house and organize party games?

b) Invest in a full Marvo The Magician outfit, attempt to saw one of the children in half to the horror of the other party guests and stomp off in a petulant fit when they fail to laugh at your magician's repartee?

c) Beg your boss to reorganize that business trip on the day of the party and cry off at the last minute?

The kids want to go on an adventure and build a camp in the woods, do you:

a) Pack some lunch, dig out your trusty old penknife and go off to the woods pretending that you need to look out for bears and other dangerous animals?

b) Dress up in full Indiana Jones mode, face camouflaged with dirt and belt bearing a hipflask of whisky, bore them with your knowledge of flora and fauna, and then start a minor forest fire with your inept attempts at building a campfire?

c) Tell them that due to current health and safety regulations you would be at risk of being sued or possibly locked up for life if you embarked on any such expedition, and make them feel really guilty for just having asked?

Your teenage son wants to go to his first rock festival, do you:

a) Lend him your tent, offer to drive him there, say you hope he has a good time, and jokingly warn him never to use the toilets?

b) Reminisce about your experiences at the Isle of Wight/ Glastonbury/Knebworth like the Uncle Albert of rock and roll and then insist on digging out your denims and going with him?

c) Say that if he wants to spend three days waist-deep in mud he could come and help you on the allotment for a change instead of lounging around in bed all weekend?

Your teenage daughter wants to go to her first nightclub, do you:

a) Give her a few quid to buy a nice outfit and offer to pick her up afterwards?
b) Insist on teaching her the Hully Gully/The Twist/The Birdie dance/Pogoing and then promptly put your back out?
c) Convince her that she will have her drink spiked, be kidnapped by a gang of evil slave traders and wake up in foreign climes as the concubine of a Third World drug trafficker?

Your toddler wants a piggyback, do you:

a) Hoick them up on your back and pretend to be a horse, clicking and neighing along the road?
b) Hoick them up on your back, pretend to be a horse running the Grand National, racing along at breakneck speed and leaping over imaginary fences until you come a cropper at Beecher's Brook and have to spend three hours in A&E?
c) Clutch your back, feign agony and suggest that Mummy do the honours as your old war wound is playing up again?

Answers

Mostly As: Well done! You are a fun dad, the kids love you for it and so do all their friends.

Mostly Bs: You may think you're a fun dad, but unfortunately you're having more fun than the kids are. Give 'em a break Dad!

Mostly Cs: Dad, you should be ashamed of yourself! You're about as much fun as Norman Bates' mum! Now shake a leg and lighten up. As Cyndi Lauper once nearly said, "Kids just wanna have fun."

Dad's Role Versus Mum's Role

Mum makes a home; dad repairs the home.

Mum offers a shoulder to cry on; dad offers a shoulder to climb on.

Mum cooks for all; dad cooks damn all.

Mum cleans the house out; dad clears out of the house.

Mum takes her sons to football; dad takes his sons on at football.

Dad rules with an iron fist; mum irons as a rule.

Dad gives help with homework; mum needs help with the housework.

Dad washes the car and walks the dog; mum washes the dog.

Dad has to lay down the law when the kids get out of hand; mum has to have a lie down.

Dad gets home from work and sees the kids; mum sees the kids and starts work.

Definitions For Mums And Dads

Bank statement:
Mums: A meaningless jumble of figures
Dads: A coronary-inducing missive on a par with a poison pen letter

Beer:
Mums: A fattening drink that makes men less attractive
Dads: An intoxicating drink that makes women more attractive

Butt:
Mums: The body part that looks bigger no matter what is worn
Male: What you kick when you want something done at work.
Also good for mooning

Children:
Mums: If you bring them up well they'll be a credit to you
Dads: If you bring them up too well they'll be a debit to your
bank balance

Commitment:
Mums: A desire to get married and raise a family
Dads: Trying not to chat up the bridesmaids at the wedding
reception

Communication:
Mums: The sharing of thoughts and feelings with one's partner
Dads: Leaving a note before suddenly taking off for a weekend
with the boys

Decorating:
Mums: A chance to make the house look nice
Dads: A fiendish choice between no weekends off for six weeks
or paying some cowboy way over the odds to do it for you

Entertainment:
Mums: A good movie, concert, play or book
Dads: Anything that can be done while drinking

Family Car:
Mums: A vehicle for ferrying children around in
Dads: A stop-gap until he can afford a Lamborghini

Flatulence:
Mums: An embarrassing by-product of digestion
Dads: An endless source of entertainment, self-expression and male bonding

Football:
Mums: A couple of hours' peace without him under her feet
Dads: A couple of hours' peace without her on his case

Garden:
Mums: A place to relax and potter about in
Dads: A place to have a quiet beer while everyone thinks he's mowing the lawn

Holiday:
Mums: A chance to put her feet up
Dads: A chance to put his credit card limit up

Housework:
Mums: A chore that makes you feel better once you've done it
Dads: A chore that makes you feel better if you can avoid it

January sales:
Mums: The more you spend, the more you're saving
Dads: The less you spend, the less you spend, full stop

Kitchen:
Mums: The hub of her empire
Dads: The nearest he's going to get to a home bar

Making love:
Mums: The greatest expression of intimacy a couple can achieve
Dads: Call it whatever you want just as long as we end up in bed

Meal:
Mums: A chore if it's at home, a treat if it's out
Dads: A God-given right if it's at home, an unnecessary expense if it's out

Means of support:
Mums: A decent bra
Dads: A decent income

Pub:
Mums: A distant memory from her single days and never thought about
Dads: A distant memory from his single days and thought about every evening about 5.30

Remote control:
Mums: A device for changing from one TV channel to another
Dads: A device for scanning through all available channels every three minutes

Repair:
Mums: Something that always needs doing round the house
Dads: To disappear – as in, "I'm going to repair to the pub." Used particularly when repairs are mentioned.

Shoes:
Mums: Endlessly fascinating objects of desire
Dads: Those things that stop your feet getting wet

Shopping:
Mums: Fun with a friend, murder with the kids
Dads: Murder with anyone

Thingy:
Mums: Any part under a car's bonnet
Dads: The strap fastener on a woman's bra

TV soaps:
Mums: A break from humdrum family life by looking at someone else's humdrum family life
Dads: Missing a crucial half-hour of TV sport

Vulnerable:
Mums: Fully opening up oneself emotionally to another
Dads: Playing cricket without first installing a protective box.

Things Dads Don't Want To Hear

I've had the kids all week; you can look after them at the weekend.

There are a couple of little jobs that need doing.

I had a little prang in the car...

I've made a list of all the things we need to buy.

It's about time you explained the facts of life to them.

I've been thinking about redecorating…

My mum's very lonely in that house all on her own now…

Ever since he saw *Billy Elliot* it's all he wants to do.

I've invited their friends for a sleepover.

Surely you can watch the kids and watch the match at the same time?

We need to talk.

I've had the scan and – it's triplets!

I've got some good news and some bad news.

I've been thinking of having a weekend away with my friend.

Jokes For Dad To Share With Mum… At His Peril

Q: How can an archaeologist tell whether a skeleton is male or female?

A: If the jawbone is worn down, he knows it's female.

Q: What is love?

A: The deluded belief that one woman is any different from another.

Q: What's the difference between PMT and BSE?

A: One's mad cow disease and the other is an agricultural problem.

Q: Why did God create Adam before he created Eve?

A: So they'd have a time for a chat.

Q: Why did God create man before he created woman?

A: He didn't want any advice.

Q: Why do men die before their wives?

A: They want to.

Q: Why do men fart more than women?

A: Women never shut up long enough to build up sufficient pressure.

Q: Why do only around 25 per cent of women get into Heaven?

A: If any more did, it wouldn't be Heaven any more.

Q: Why do women close their eyes while making love?

A: They simply can't bear to see a man having a good time.

Q: Why do women live longer than men?

A: They don't have wives.

Q: Why are middle-aged women like MTV?

A: They only get turned on about once a month, then you've had enough after about 15 minutes.

Q: Why do women put on make-up and perfume?

A: Because they're ugly and they smell.

Things Not To Say To Your Wife During An Argument

Don't you have some laundry to do or something?

Well this is a fine example to set to the kids.

Couldn't we do this via email or something?

What's the point in arguing? You're always right anyway.

It looks like someone had an extra bowl of bitch flakes this morning!

You know what the doctor said about your blood pressure...

Oh, hold on a minute – I get it. What time of the month is it?

Of course we disagree – you're a woman!

Now look, you're clearly just messing around. We both know that thing isn't loaded.

Are you going to lower your voice or shall we just invite the neighbours in and let them have a ringside seat?

Can we finish this later? The football's just starting.

Why can't we discuss this calmly like adults?

You look so gorgeous when you get angry.

Don't pull that face! You know it gives you instant wrinkles!

Why do you women always get so hysterical?

You're just upset because your bottom is beginning to spread.

Your mother was like this when she went through the menopause too.

I'm going to the pub now and when I return I expect a written apology waiting for me.

Stop shouting at me! You're making your cellulite wobble!

Hush now, sweetie! The man of the house has spoken!

Sorry! I got distracted thinking about how good the sex after this argument is going to be!

Words Of Wisdom On How To Get On With Mum

Dad says men and women will never get on because they both have fundamentally different views about sex and relationships. Women want a relationship without the complication of unnecessary sex, while men want sex without the complication of an unnecessary relationship.

In order to be happy with a man you have to try to understand him a lot and love him a little. In order to be happy with a woman you have to love her a lot and not try to understand her at all.

> **"Any man today who returns from work, sinks into a chair and calls for his pipe is a man with an appetite for danger."**
> **Bill Cosby**

Men and women should try and put their differences behind them. Unfortunately this is usually very uncomfortable unless they are both contortionists.

There are seven ages of woman: baby, child, girl, young woman, young woman, young woman and young woman.

There are only two occasions when a man is unable to understand a woman: before he gets married and after he gets married.

You only need to do two things to keep your wife happy. Firstly, let her think she is having her own way, secondly let her have it.

You should never tell a woman you are not worthy of her love. She already knows.

Dad says he hasn't spoken to Mum in five years. He says he doesn't like to interrupt her.

> **"Men and women belong to different species and communication between them is still in its infancy."**
> **Bill Cosby**

Dad says if a man steals your wife, there is no better way to get your own back on him than by letting him keep her.

Important advice for all married men. Never argue with a wife who will be packing your parachute.

> **"Male menopause is a lot more fun than female menopause. With female menopause you gain weight and get hot flushes. With male menopause you get to date young girls and drive motorcycles or sports cars."**
> **Rita Rudner**

Nobody will ever win the battle of the sexes. There's too much fraternising with the enemy.

Women are always going on about how they think they're smarter than men, but it's not true. Have you ever see a man wearing a shirt with buttons going down the back?

Women blame men for lying to them, but really it's all their fault. They ask too many questions.

> **"Women don't want to hear what you think. Women want to hear what they think – in a deeper voice."**
> **Bill Cosby**

Hold on! Dad's Just Thought Of A Few More Jokes About Women...

A woman is an unpredictable creature. Before marriage, she expects a man; after marriage, she suspects him; and after death, she respects him.

A radical feminist speaker was delivering a speech. Hoping to rouse up the women in the crowd she asked, "So tell me, where would man be today if it were not for woman?" She waited a moment, looked around the room and asked the question again. "Where would man be today if it were not for woman?" From the back of the room came a voice, "He'd be in the Garden of Eden eating strawberries."

According to a recent study the average male will say 35,000 words a day in conversation while a female says only 30,000. Dad says that unfortunately, by the time he gets home from work, he's got through his entire quota while Mum has apparently yet to start on hers.

An aeroplane runs into trouble and the captain announces there's nothing they can do, the plane is going to crash. The passengers are terrified, but one woman leaps up and says, "If I have to die, I want to die feeling like a real woman." She takes off her clothes and says, "Right! Is there a man on this plane who wants to make me feel like a real woman?" "Yes," says a man getting up and taking off his shirt. "Here! Iron this would you?"

How to satisfy a woman every time: lick, paw, ogle, caress, praise, pamper, relish, savour, massage, empathize, serenade, compliment, support, dig, feed, tantalize, bathe, humour, placate, stimulate, lubricate, stroke, console, bark, purr, hug, baste, marinate, coddle, excite, pacify, tattoo, protect, phone, correspond, anticipate, nuzzle, smooch, toast, minister to, forgive, sacrifice, ply, accessorize, leave, return, beseech, sublimate, entertain, charm, lug, drag, crawl, tunnel, show equality for, oblige, fascinate, attend, implore, bawl, shower, shave, ululate, trust, dip, twirl, dive, grovel, ignore, defend, milk, coax, clothe, straddle, melt, brag, acquiesce, prevail, super collide, fuse, fizz, rationalise, detoxify, sanctify, help, acknowledge, polish, upgrade, spoil, embrace, delouse, accept, butter-up, hear, understand, beg, plead, borrow, steal, climb, swim, hold her hair while she's puking in the toilet, nurse, resuscitate, repair, patch, respect, entertain, calm, allay, kill for, die for, dream of, promise, exceed, deliver, tease, flirt, enlist, torch, pine, wheedle, cajole, murmur, snuggle, elevate, enervate, alleviate, serve, rub, rib, salve, bite, taste, nibble, gratify, take her to Funky Town, scuttle like a crab on the ocean floor of her existence, diddle, doodle, hokey-cokey, hanky-panky, flip, flop, fly, swing, slip, slide, slather, mollycoddle, squeeze, moisturize, humidify, lather, tingle, slam-dunk, keep on rockin' in the free world, wet, slicken, undulate, gelatinise, brush, tingle, dribble, drip, dry, knead, fluff, fold, ingratiate, indulge, wow, dazzle, amaze, flabbergast, enchant, idolize and worship, and then go back, Jack, and do it again.

How to satisfy a man every time: Turn up naked.

In the beginning, God created the earth and then he rested. Then God created man and then he rested. Then God created woman. And since then, neither God nor man has rested.

A man is walking along the beach when he finds an old bottle which he picks up, pulls the cork out of and looks inside. Suddenly out pops a genie who tells him, "Oh great master, thank you for freeing me from the bottle. Now in return I must grant you three wishes." "Wow," says the man. "Well, I've often fantasized about this so I've got my three wishes all ready for you. First, I want you to pay ten billion pounds into my bank account for me." "Your will shall be done," says the genie and suddenly there is a flash of light and a bank statement showing his new balance appears in the man's hand. "Amazing," says the man, "OK. How about a brand new red Ferrari?" "Your will shall be done," says the genie, there's another flash of light and there's the man's brand new red Ferrari. "This is great," says the man. "OK. Last wish. I want you to make me completely irresistible to every single woman in the entire world." "Your will shall be done," says the genie, there's yet another flash of light and the man finds he has been magically transformed into a box of chocolates.

In a recent scientific study a hundred men were each given 12 pints of beer. After they drank the beer the men were all observed to gain weight, lose the ability to drive, to become emotional, talk excessively without making sense and refused to back down or apologize if they were shown to be wrong in any argument. The scientists running the study concluded that beer must contain female hormones.

Things Wives Say And What They Actually Mean

Be honest, do you like this outfit?
Lie your head off convincingly or you're a dead man.

Fine
The word women use to end an argument when they are right and you need to shut up.

Five minutes
If she is getting dressed, this means half an hour. Five minutes is only five minutes if you have just been given five more minutes to watch the football before helping around the house.

Go ahead then
This is a dare, not permission. Don't do it.

I don't really want anything for Christmas
If you take this literally you're dead.

I've got nothing to wear
Dust off your wallet, mate!

Loud sigh
This is not actually a word, but a non-verbal statement often misunderstood by men. It means she thinks you are an idiot and wonders why she is wasting her time standing there arguing with you over "nothing".

Nothing
This is the calm before the storm. This means "something" and you should be on your toes. When the answer is "nothing" then it's usually the start of something that will invariably end with "fine".

Oh, you wouldn't understand
You are a man and therefore technically incapable of grasping anything that isn't to do with cars, football or beer.

Sit down, I'll make you a cup of tea
I've crashed the car/spent all your money/am having an affair (or possibly all three).

Thanks
A woman is thanking you. Do not question it. Just say, "That's all right" and be grateful.

That's OK
One of the most dangerous statements that a woman can make to a man. "That's OK" means that she wants to think long and hard before deciding how and when you will pay for your mistake.

We need to talk
You need to listen!

The 'Car Way' Of Gauging The Length Of A relationship

Trying to impress the woman: the man unlocks and opens the door, waits for her to get inside, closes her door behind her.

Dating: the guy unlocks her door and then goes around to his side to get in.

Engaged: The guy opens his door leans over and unlocks her door and opens it.

Married: The guy gets in to the driver's seat, unlocks the doors, and says, "Aren't you getting in?"

The Geography Of Woman

Between 15 and 16, a woman is like China; developing fast with a lot of potential, but as yet still not free or open. Between 17 and 18, a woman is like Hawaii; young, hot and tantalizing, but capable of giving severe burns if caught in the wrong place at the wrong time. Between 18 and 21, a woman is like Africa; half-discovered, half-wild and naturally beautiful. Between 21 and 30, a woman is like the USA; well-developed and open to trade, especially for someone with cash. Between 30 and 40, a woman is like India; very hot, relaxed and convinced of her own beauty. Between 41 and 50, a woman is like Great Britain; with a glorious and all-conquering past. Between 51 and 55, a woman is like Germany; lost the war and haunted by past mistakes. Between 56 and 60, a woman is like Iraq; needs massive reconstruction. Between 61 and 70, a woman is like

Russia; very wide and with borders that are now unpatrolled. Between 70 and 75, a woman is like Mongolia; with a glorious and all-conquering past, but alas no future. After 75, women become like Australia; everyone knows where it is, but no one wants to go down there.

Two dads are talking about their favourite Hollywood actress, Angelina Jolie. "Still," says one, "if you took away Angelina's beautiful eyes, magnificent hair, perfect features and amazing shapely body, what would you be left with?" The other thinks for a moment and says, "My wife."

Dad's Guide To Being Politically Correct So As Not To Annoy The Missus

She doesn't TALK TOO MUCH she is VERBALLY EXPANSIVE.

She doesn't EAT TOO MUCH she suffers from CALORIE RETENTION.

She isn't a SLOB she has CHORE AVERSION SYNDROME.

She isn't a TYRANT she is CHALLENGINGLY SINGLE-MINDED.

She doesn't DRINK TOO MUCH she has A LOW ALCOHOL TOLERANCE.

She isn't TOO SOFT ON THE KIDS she has CONFRONTATIONAL DISCIPLINE ISSUES.

She isn't DEMANDING she has A FULLY-DEVELOPED UNDERSTANDING OF PERSONAL TARGETS.

She doesn't have A FABULOUS BODY she is COSMETICALLY SATISFIED.

She isn't a BAD DRIVER she has OTHERLY DEFINED MOTORING SKILLS.

She isn't a BIG SPENDER she is UPWARDLY MOBILE WITHIN A FINANCIALLY RESTRICTED FRAMEWORK.

Her breasts will never SAG they will LOSE THEIR VERTICAL HOLD.

She does not CUT YOU OFF she becomes HORIZONTALLY INACCESSIBLE.

She does not SLUR HER WORDS when drunk she is VERBALLY DYSLEXIC.

She does not HATE SPORTS ON TV she is ATHLETICALLY BIASED.

She does not have A GREAT BUM she is GLUTEUS TO THE MAXIMUS.

She does not have a KILLER BODY she is TERMINALLY ATTRACTIVE.

She does not have BIG HAIR she is ABUNDANTLY AEROSOLED.

She does not have BIG BREASTS her CUPS RUNNETH OVER.

She does not SHAVE HER LEGS she indulges in TEMPORARY STUBBLE REDUCTION.

She does not SHOP TOO MUCH she is OVERLY SUSCEPTIBLE TO MARKETING PLOYS.

She does not SNORE she is NASALLY CONVERSATIONAL.

She does not SUNBATHE she indulges in SOLAR ENHANCEMENT.

She does not WEAR TOO MUCH MAKE-UP she is FULLY COSMETICIZED.

She doesn't get PMT she is HORMONALLY ASSERTIVE.

She is not a BAD COOK she has MICROWAVE MANAGEMENT SKILLS.

She is not a GOSSIP she has WIDE SOCIAL NETWORKING SKILLS.

She is not MOANER she is VOCALLY ASSERTIVE.

She is not FRIGID she is THERMALLY INCOMPATIBLE.

She is not HOOKED ON SOAP OPERAS she is A MATURE DRAMA STUDENT.

She is not TOO SKINNY she is REFUSING TO BE DICTATED TO BY THE CORPORATE FOOD INDUSTRY.

She is not TOO FAT she is REFUSING TO CONFORM TO FEMALE STEREOTYPES.

She will never GAIN WEIGHT she will become A METABOLIC UNDERACHEIVER.

You do not ASK HER TO DANCE you REQUEST A NON-COMMITTAL RHYTHMIC EXPERIENCE.

Splitting Up

There was a dad who, many years ago, found himself muttering a few words in the church and got himself married. A few years later he found himself muttering something in his sleep and got himself divorced.

Two dads are talking after one has just got divorced. The first buys his friend a drink and tells him, "Losing a wife must be very hard." "You're right," says the second. "In fact I found it damn near impossible!"

Mum and Dad have to go and see a marriage guidance counsellor about the state of their relationship. In the end the counsellor can't understand how either of them can bear to live with the other. "I know," says Mum. "In fact the only reason we've stayed married this long is because neither of us wanted to be given custody of the children."

"Mommy would never divorce Daddy. He's just like one of the family."
Bill Keane

A man becomes involved in a major custody battle. His wife doesn't want him any more and his mother won't have him back.

A judge says to a mother in a family law case: "Do you understand that you have sworn to tell the truth?" "Yes, I do," says the mother. "And do you understand what will happen if you are not truthful?" asks the judge. "Yes," says the mother. "I get everything I want."

A judge says to a father in a divorce hearing: "Do you have anything to offer this court before I issue my judgement?" "No, Your Honour," says the father. "My lawyer's already taken it all."

A couple are going through a divorce and have to go to court to resolve the issue of custody of the children. In court the mother tells the judge that she should keep the children because she was the one who brought them into the world. The judge thinks that this is a good point and turns to the father to see if he has any response. The dad thinks for a moment, then says, "Your Honour, look at it a different way. If I was buying a chocolate bar from a machine and I put 50 pence in the slot and a chocolate bar dropped out of the bottom, who does that chocolate bar belong to? Me or the machine?"

A couple decide to get divorced despite the fact they're both in their nineties. Their friends can't believe it. "How can you do this?" they ask. "After more than 70 years of marriage what's the point of getting a divorce now?" "Well," says the couple, "to be honest with you, we've hated the sight of each other for years and wanted to separate for a long time, but didn't want to go through with it till the kids had died."

During a divorce case, a judge tells a father, "I have reviewed this case very carefully and have decided to let your wife have £2,000 a month." "Why that's incredibly generous of you," says the dad. "Do you know what? I might even chip in with a pound or two myself."

During a divorce hearing a judge asks a mother on what grounds she wants to divorce her husband. "Infidelity," says the mum. "Really?" says the judge. "And do you have any evidence for that?" "Yes I do," says the mum. "I'm pretty certain he's not the father of three of our kids."

A dad goes to his wife and tells her that he has decided it would be better if they separate. "You want a divorce?" she says in astonishment. "After all these years together? We've been through so much and for better and for worse I've stuck with you. What about when your business was ruined, who was with you then? What about when you had that heart attack, who was there at your side? When your dad died in that freak accident, who was with you then? What about when the house was destroyed in that earthquake, who was there with you then?" "That's just it," says the dad, "I've finally realized after all these years, you're a bloody jinx!"

Why Mum Isn't Allowed To Do DIY (According to Dad)

When she was asked to change a fuse she took it back to the shop.

She won't use a ladder when there's a perfectly good chair to stand on.

When the plumber told her the tap needed a new washer she got out the Zanussi catalogue.

She thinks a mallet is a sort of ornamental doorstop.

When the smoke alarm stopped working she deliberately burnt some toast to try and get it going again.

She took the Pollyfilla back to the shop because it was too soft to be any use in filling holes in the wall.

She bought a self-assembly unit, laid all the bits out on the floor and stood waiting for it to assemble itself.

She took a bayonet-style light bulb back to the shop and asked if she could have a round one instead.

She insisted on wearing her anorak while decorating because the paint tin said, "one coat required".

When the nails she bought weren't long enough she went back and asked for extensions.

Dad's Football Definitions

Ball: Round object used by referees to entice players into committing fouls

Defender: Player whose function is to commit fouls just outside the penalty area

Fans: Two large-ish groups of abusive amateur referees

Football: A game consisting of 22 skilled players, one impartial referee, two eagle–eyed referee's assistants and one stupid ball

Offside: A Bermuda Triangle-like area of the pitch towards which "innocent" players will inevitably be drawn

Scoring: Moment when 11 men spontaneously start dancing and kissing each other, regardless of any injuries they may recently have suffered, while 11 others suddenly droop like wallflowers

Striker: Faultless, overpaid, box hogging layabout who only misses the goal when he is fed a bad ball

Team mate: Another obstacle it is necessary to dribble around

Survival Tips for Dads

Always take on any available overtime at work – it's easier than trying to supervise the kids at bathtime.

Teach the kids to drive as young as possible or you'll be an unpaid taxi service as soon as they learn to refuse to walk.

Equip the garden shed with beer fridge, dartboard and a small supply of food – you're going to be spending a lot of time out there in the years to come.

If you get a pay rise keep it quiet and ask for it to be paid into a secret account – it's the only way you'll ever have any money.

Even if you don't like sport, become a fervent supporter and it's your passport to freedom every once in a while.

Pretend to have intermittent deafness – it'll come in handy when the kids want money or the wife wants to go shopping.

Buy a Robin Reliant then none of your teenagers will ever want to borrow it.

Pretend that you really like rap music and then it'll put the kids off it and they'll never play it round the house.

On the kids' birthdays fork out for a trip to the cinema or something – at least it'll save your house from being trashed by a horde of hyperactive six-year-olds.

Invent a new condition called something like "infantaphobia" and explain to your wife that you will develop a serious illness if you have to look after the kids for more than half an hour at a time.

Reasons It's Good To Be A Bloke

A bit of excess weight round the middle does not make you invisible to the opposite sex.

A two-week holiday only requires only one suitcase.

All your orgasms are real.

Car mechanics tell you the truth.

Chocolate is just another snack.

Christmas shopping for 25 relatives can be accomplished on Christmas Eve, in 40 minutes.

Hairdressers don't rob you blind.

Grey hair and wrinkles add character.

Hot wax never comes near your pubic area.

If another man shows up at a party in the same outfit, you just might become lifelong friends.

If someone forgets to invite you to something, he can still be your friend.

If something mechanical doesn't work, you can hit it with a hammer and throw it across the room.

If you don't call your mate when you say you will, he won't tell your friends you've changed.

If you're 34 and single, nobody notices.

Robbie Williams doesn't live in your universe.

Movie nudity is virtually always female.

New shoes don't squash, blister or cut your feet.

Nobody stops telling a good dirty joke when you walk in the room.

None of your co-workers has the power to make you cry.

Old friends don't care if we've lost or gained weight.

People never stare at your chest when you're talking to them.

Phone conversations are over in 30 seconds flat.

The garage is all yours.

The remote control is all yours.

The same hairstyle lasts for years, maybe decades.

Wedding plans take care of themselves.

With 400 million sperm per shot, you could double the earth's population in 15 tries, at least in theory.

You can be showered and ready in ten minutes.

You can drop by to see a friend without having to bring a little gift.

You can go to a public toilet without a support group.

You can open all your own jars.

You can sit with your knees apart no matter what you are wearing.

You can wear one pair of shoes all year round for any occasion.

You can whip your shirt off on a hot day.

You can write your name in the snow.

You do the same work, but get more pay.

You don't care if someone is talking about you behind your back.

You don't give a toss if someone doesn't notice your new haircut.

You don't have to remember everyone's birthdays and anniversaries.

You don't have to shave below your neck.

You don't insist on pinching bits of other people's desserts.

You get extra credit for the slightest act of thoughtfulness.

You have freedom of choice when it comes to growing a moustache.

You have one mood, all the time.

You never have to clean the toilet.

You only suffer from PMT indirectly.

Your last name stays put.

Your mates can be trusted never to trap you with, "So... notice anything different?"

Your underwear is £8 for a three-pack.

Dad's Definitions Of Household Appliances

Cooker: Magical device that not only cooks meals without human assistance but also cleans itself

Dishwasher: It takes away the drudgery of having to do washing up (though how the hell it gets the crockery and cutlery back into the cupboards is anyone's guess)

Food mixer: An over-promoted fork

Freezer: Handy for resting cup of tea on when working in the garage

Fridge: Home bar (can also store food apparently)

Hairdryer: A distant memory from when you had hair

Iron: It must have been invented by a woman – no man yet has managed to master it

Juicer: For people too lazy to buy their orange juice in cartons

Microwave oven: Why on earth do women moan about cooking when they can do everything in two minutes in this baby? OK, it's tricky stacking up four plates of food, but....

Self-cleaning oven: Aren't all ovens self-cleaning?

Toaster: Another one that must have been invented by a woman – major design fault: it makes one hell of a mess when you try making cheese on toast

Tumble drier: Just big enough to fit a small child after it's been splashing around in puddles and getting its clothes all wet

Vacuum cleaner: Handy for cleaning out the inside of the car

Washing machine: Utterly fabulous device that not only collects clothes from floor all over house, but washes them and has them back in your wardrobe a day or so later

Waste-disposal unit: Plughole with teeth

Dads' Guide To The Toolbox For Mums

Screwdrivers are to be used for tightening or loosening screws, not as levers for opening boxes, tins and jars or for making holes in the garden to plant seeds in.

Hammers are to be used for hammering in nails and not as temporary paperweights or doorstops for the shed door.

Saws are to be used for sawing wood and not for carving up old cardboard boxes that are too big to go in the recycling bin.

Electric drills are to be used for drilling holes and not for scaring away next-door's cat who is pooing in the garden.

A spirit level is to be used to establish whether a surface is level and not to keep the baby amused while you get on with cooking dinner.

A vice is not one of dad's bad habits.

Spanners are meant for tightening or loosening nuts, not for use as surrogate hammers when you can't find the real one.

A tin of paint is to be used for decorating, not as a doorstop to get some air into the kitchen during hot weather.

The tape measure is for measuring things around the house, not dad's expanding waistline.

The awl is for making holes in pieces of wood, not for getting the milk out of coconuts won at the funfair.

The monkey wrench is not a last resort opener for getting a difficult cork out of a bottle of fizzy wine.

Quotes From Great Dads Of The World - Homer Simpson

Operator! Give me the number for 911!

What do we need a psychiatrist for? We know our kid is nuts.

I think the saddest day of my life was when I realized I could beat my Dad at most things – and Bart experienced that at the age of four.

> **Bart: I am through with working. Working is for chumps.**
> **Homer: Son, I'm proud of you! I was twice your age when I figured that out.**

All my life I've had one dream: to achieve my many goals.

All right, brain. You don't like me and I don't like you, but let's just do this and I can get back to killing you with beer.

Don't worry head. The computer will do all the thinking from now on.

Dear Lord, the Gods have been good to me. As an offering, I present these milk and cookies. If you wish me to eat them instead, please give me no sign whatsoever... Thy will be done.

Facts are meaningless. You could use facts to prove anything that's even remotely true!

I bet Einstein turned himself into all sorts of colours before he invented the light bulb.

I think Smithers picked me because of my motivational skills. Everyone says they have to work a lot harder when I'm around.

> **Bart: What religion are you?**
> **Homer: You know, the one with all the well-**
> **meaning rules that don't work out in real**
> **life. Uh... Christianity.**

I want my answers now or I want them eventually.

Oh, so they have Internet on computers now!

I hope I didn't brain my damage.

Dads And Little Kids

This is the fun stage.
   In theory.
   When they were babies you hardly knew what to do with them, now they're a bit bigger you can play games with them, take them out to the park or the seaside, and now of course they can talk to you. They'll say thing like, "Who says I have to?" and "Your breakfast isn't as nice as Mummy's," or "Why don't I get as much pocket money as my friends?"
   But you still love them – even when they've just spilt a gooey drink over your new laptop or thought your car would look even better with stripes painted down the sides or when they've just flooded the bathroom. At least babies are contained most of the time. Little kids just seem to be everywhere at once. Imagine

having six of them – pulling out your treasured DVD collection, tormenting the cat, digging up your tomato plants, playing with the set of shears you've just sharpened, pulling each other's hair, screaming the place down and leaving a trail of brightly-coloured sticky mess wherever they go like psychedelic snails. In fact, you don't need six of them, that's what it feels like when you've just got the one.

Still, life would be dull without them wouldn't it?

Oh, for a bit of dullness now and then!

Mummy catches her little boy using a very naughty word one day. "That's a very rude thing to say," says Mummy. "I don't like you using words like that. Where did you hear it?" "Daddy said it," says the boy. Later on Mummy has a word with Daddy to tell him to mind his language when the children are listening. "Oh well," says Daddy. "At least he doesn't know what it means." "Yes I do," pipes up a little voice, "It means the car won't start."

A couple and their small son move from the country to a new house in the middle of the city. The morning after the move the little boy wakes them up early so they get him dressed and tell him to play outside in the garden for a while. A little while later the boy comes running in saying, "Daddy! Daddy! You'll never guess! Everybody here has doorbells and they all work!"

A little boy was getting fed up being told what to do by everybody. In the end he went to his dad and asked, "Dad, when will I be old enough to do what I want?" "I don't know, son," answered Dad, "Nobody's lived that long yet."

A dad is in church with his nine-year-old son. Half way through the service the boy starts to feel ill and pulls his dad's sleeve. "Dad," he says. "You've got to take me home now! I'm feeling really ill." "Now stop that," says Dad. "I'm not taking you anywhere. It's not long 'til end of the service. I'm sure you can wait 'til then." "But, Dad, I really think I'm going to throw up any second!" "In that case you better run outside, go round the back of the church and throw up behind the bushes," says Dad. A few minutes later the boy is back in his seat. "That was quick," says Dad. "I thought you were going to be sick." "I was," says the boy. "But how did you get round to the bushes in that time?" "No need," says the little boy. "I got to the back of the church and I noticed they had a special box right by the door with a big sign on it saying, 'For the sick'."

A little boy is out with his mother one day in a cafe and embarrasses her by asking loudly if he can go for a wee wee. His mother tells him, "Don't shout out like that. In future, if you want a wee wee just say, 'I want a whisper' and then I'll know what you mean." A few days later the boy goes into the living room and finds his dad has fallen asleep in front of the TV. The little boy gives his dad a prod and wakes him up. Drowsily the father asks him what he wants. "I want a whisper," says the little boy. "All right," says Dad. "Go on then! Whisper in my ear!"

A young dad was getting ready for work one morning while his two-year-old daughter was playing on the bedroom floor. Then she said, "Dad, look at this," and stuck out one of her fingers. To carry on the fun, Dad grabbed her hand and stuck her fingers in his mouth saying, "Daddy is going to eat your fingers!" Then he pretended to eat her fingers before getting his jacket out of the wardrobe. When he turned round, his little girl was sitting on the floor looking at her finger and crying. Dad said, "Sorry darling, I didn't hurt your fingers did I?" "No," she said. "But, Daddy, where has my bogey gone?"

A telephone salesman phones a house and a four-year-old girl answers. The salesman says, "May I speak to your mother please?" And the girl says, "No. She isn't here." So the salesman says, "OK. Could I speak to your father? Is he there?" "No," says the girl. "Well, is anyone else there?" asks the salesman. "My sister is," says the girl. "OK," says the salesman. "In that case may I speak to her then?" "Hold on," says the girl. A long silence follows before the girl picks up the receiver again and says, "Hello?" "Ah!" says the salesman. "It's you again. I thought you said you were going to go and get your sister." "I tried," says the girl. "The problem is that I can't lift her out of her play pen."

TRUE STORY

John Cleese and Connie Booth's daughter was present for the filming of the Black Knight scene in the film *Monty Python and the Holy Grail* in which her dad, as the Black Knight, continues to pick a fight with King Arthur despite Arthur lopping his arms and legs off one by one with a sword. The little girl watched all this going on before commenting, "Daddy doesn't like that man, does he?"

A dad takes his son to the doctor's because the boy has a toy car shoved up his nose. All the while the doctor is attempting to remove the car, the dad keeps saying, "I just don't know how he did it!" Finally the doctor manages to remove the little car and the two leave. A few hours later, the dad comes back. This time the dad has the toy car shoved up HIS nose. He tells the doctor, "Now I know how he did it!"

A little boy greets his grandmother who has come to stay and tells her, "I'm really happy you've come to see us, Grandma. Now Daddy's going to do the trick he has been promising us." "Oh yes," says the grandmother looking intrigued. "And what trick is that, dear?" "Well," says the little boy, "I overheard Daddy say to Mummy that if you ever came to stay with us again he would 'climb up the bloody wall'!"

> **"I hurt my back the other day. I was playing piggyback with my six-year-old nephew and I fell off."**
>
> **Tommy Cooper**

A vicar is visiting a primary school and asks the children if they say their prayers at night. One little boy tells him that his father says a special prayer about him every evening. "Oh really?" says the vicar, looking pleased. "And what does your father say?" The boy answers, "He says, 'Thank God the little bastard's in bed at last!'"

Two primary school children are talking. One asks the other, "What does your Daddy do for a living?" "He's a lawyer," says the second. "Honest?" asks the first. "No," says the second. "The normal kind."

A little boy goes away to summer camp and after a few days writes home, and says, "Dear Mum and Dad, please send some food. All they serve here are meals."

A little boy was being driven by his dad past a church with a large sign outside it. The boy read the sign and asked, "Is that true? Does God really come from Ikea?" "Why do you ask that, son?" asked Dad. "Because," said the boy, "that sign just said we could go into that church and see the Assembly of God."

A priest is walking down a country lane when he sees a young boy struggling to get a load of hay back onto a cart after it has fallen off into the road. "That looks like hard work, my son," says the priest. "Why not have a rest for a moment and then I'll help you." "No thank you," says the boy. "My dad wouldn't like that." "Oh don't be silly," says the priest. "Surely your dad wouldn't mind you having a rest for a minute. Come and have a drink of water." "No really," says the boy. "My dad will be very cross if I don't keep working." Well," says the priest, "it sounds to me like your father is a real slave driver. I'm going to have words him about this. Where can I find him?" "He's underneath this pile of hay," says the boy.

"A new father quickly learns that his child invariably comes to the bathroom at precisely the times when he's in there, as if he needed company. The only way for this father to be certain of bathroom privacy is to shave at the gas station."

Bill Cosby

A vicar is walking down the street one day when he notices a little boy trying to press a doorbell on a house across the street. But because the boy is still quite small the doorbell is too high for him to press it. He struggles and jumps, but is still unable to reach. After watching the boy's vain attempts for a minute, the vicar walks across the street and approaches him. "Here, let me help," he says and gives the doorbell a good loud ring. He bends down to the little boy's level and smiles, then asks, "And now what young man?" The boy grins and says, "Now we run!"

After putting their four-year-old son Billy to bed one night his parents heard screaming and crying coming from his room. They hurried in and tried to calm him down to ask what was wrong. Eventually, through his sobs, he managed to tell them that he had swallowed a penny and that he was sure he was going to die. Nothing his parents said seemed to reassure him that everything was going to be all right so his dad quietly took a penny from his pocket and pretended to pull it from young Billy's ear. Almost immediately the boy cheered up and looked relieved. He then suddenly grabbed the penny from his dad's hand and swallowed it, saying, "Go on, Dad! Do it again!"

Dad asks his little boy, "Son, did you really put a slug in Auntie Doris's bed?" "Yes I did," says the boy. "Why, son? Why did you do such a thing?" asks Dad. "Sorry, Dad," says the boy. "I couldn't find my snake."

Dad gets fed up with his youngest son weeing in the bath. "Oi!" says Dad. "Stop that now! It's unhygienic to wee in the bath. And what's more, you could at least wait until I get out."

> **"I was kidnapped and they sent a ransom note to my parents. And my father has bad reading habits, so he gets into bed at night with the ransom note, and he read half of it, and he got drowsy and fell asleep."**
>
> **Woody Allen**

Henry and Lucy are only ten years old, but they are in love. One day they decide that they want to get married, so Henry goes to Lucy's dad to ask permission. Henry summons up his courage and says "Mr Burroughs, Lucy and I are in love and I want to ask you for her hand in marriage." Thinking that this is rather cute and old fashioned, Mr Burroughs decides to go along with it for a while and says, "Well, young man, you're only ten years old, where will you both live?" Henry, who has obviously been thinking about this in advance says, "In Lucy's room. It's bigger than mine and it should do us both nicely." Surprised, but rather charmed by this reply, Mr Burroughs says with a smile, "But what are you going to live on? You're not old enough to get a job, and you'll have to support your wife." Henry seems to have this worked out too. "We've got our pocket money... Lucy gets two pounds a week and I get four pounds a week. That's about 24 pounds a month and that should do us just fine." By this time Mr Burroughs is rather taken aback that this young boy has planned it all out to such a degree. So he tries to think of a question that will stump young Henry and end the conversation. After a few moments Mr Burroughs says, "Well young man, it seems like you've got it all worked out. There's just one more thing you need to consider: how will you manage if you have some little children of your own?" Henry just shrugs his shoulders and says, "Well, Mr Burroughs, we've been lucky up till now..."

> "I remember the time I was kidnapped and they sent a piece of my finger to my father. He said he wanted more proof."
>
> **Rodney Dangerfield**

Four-year-old George says, "Dad! Can I have a piece of your chewing gum please?" "Sorry, son," replies Dad. "This is that special breath freshening gum. I think it will probably be too strong for you." "No it won't, Dad," says little George flexing his arm. "Look at my big muscles!"

TRUE STORY

In the USA a former Marine got a job working for the United Parcel Service. He and his wife bought their four-year-old boy a present of two teddy bears. The two toy bears were dressed in the two uniforms that his Dad had worn – United Parcel Service and the full military uniform of the Marines. The little boy was confused as to the significance of this. So his dad found a photograph of himself in his old military uniform. "See," he said, showing the little boy the picture and then pointing to the bear. "That's Daddy." The little boy was more confused than ever. "What?" he said. "You mean you used to be a bear?"

Little Cameron was watching his dad in the garden one day while he was making a rabbit hutch out of some old wood. Meanwhile his mother was indoors making them all a sandwich. After about half an hour Cameron came indoors crying. "What's the matter?" his mother asked. "Daddy hit his thumb with the hammer," said little Cameron. "That's nothing for you to cry about now is it?" said mum. "Daddy will be fine, and I'm sure that when it happened it looked quite funny, like something from *You've Been Framed*. I don't know why you didn't laugh when it happened." "That's the problem," said Cameron. "I did!"

One evening Mum was out at her yoga class and Dad was cooking dinner. Just as it was almost ready his five-year-old son came downstairs crying. Dad picked him up and said, "What's wrong, little man?" The boy said, "Dad, I just tidied my room!" "Well done!" said Dad. "Your mum will be really pleased with you when she gets home, but why are you crying?" The boy stopped sobbing for a moment and said, "Because I still can't find my pet snake!"

> **"When I was a kid I got no respect. The time I was kidnapped, and the kidnappers sent my parents a note, they said, 'We want 5,000 dollars or you'll see your kid again.'"**
> **Rodney Dangerfield**

Little Jason's dad went to pay at the reception desk in the dentist's, but was shocked when he saw the bill. "I don't understand it," he complained. "I thought his treatment would only cost £20, but you've charged me £100." "It is usually £20, sir," agreed the assistant, "but Jason screamed so loudly that four of our other patients ran away."

When the Robinson family moved into their new house, their aunt Hilda came to visit and asked five-year-old Petronella how she liked the new place. "It's really nice," she said. "I've got my own room, Timothy has his own room, and even little Lily has her own room. But poor old Mum is still in with Dad."

"My parents finally realize that I'm kidnapped. They snap into action immediately: they rent out my room. The ransom note says for my father to leave a thousand dollars in a hollow tree in New Jersey. He has no trouble raising a thousand dollars, but he gets a hernia carrying the hollow tree."

Woody Allen

One evening while his mum and dad were out a little boy was showing some family photos to the babysitter. He pointed out a nice picture of his whole family, and she told him how grown up and handsome he looked in it. He shook his head and said, "No, my mum doesn't like that one. She said she wants to have it blown up."

TRUE STORY

A man was coming home from a trip when there was a severe lightning storm. By the time he finally arrived back and was about to climb into bed it was two in the morning. He discovered his two children had got into bed with his wife because they had been scared by the storm, so he had to go and sleep in the guest bedroom. The next day, he told his kids that they could sleep with their mum if they were frightened, but if he was expected home that night, they should try and stay in their own beds. The kids said OK. After his next trip a few weeks later, his wife and the children came to pick him up from the airport and, as he entered the waiting area, his son came running up and announced loudly in front of all the other passengers, "Dad! I've got some good news! Nobody slept with Mummy while you were away this time!"

Things Dads Learn From Their Kids

Mums are always right – even when they're wrong.

If you complain about Mum's cooking she'll expect you to do it.

A bunch of flowers is a cheap price to pay for a quiet life.

If you can prove that you're absolutely hopeless at doing a simple task like putting away your clothes Mum will do it for you.

How to work the computer.

How to send a text message.

Bedtime Stories – Dad Style

Goldilocks And The Three Beers

Pizza Pan And Wendy Burger

Little-Read Riding Hood

Harry Potter And The Half-Cut Prince

The Gruff Hello

Alice's Adventures In Pizzaland

Peter And The Wolf-Whistle

The Wonderful Wizened Old Ozzy

The Tail Of An Eaten Rabbit

Snack And The Beans Talk

More Slightly Inappropriate Works Of Literature That Dads Might Be Tempted To Read To Little Ones At Bedtime
(But Really Shouldn't)

Haynes Car Guide 2008

The World According To Jeremy Clarkson

The Collected Works Of Sven Hassell

The Viz Annual

The Good Pub Guide

Readers Digest DIY Manual (including CD Rom)

Hitler 1889 – 1936: Hubris by Ian Kershaw

I Was Keith Richards' Drugs Dealer by Tony Sanchez

The Instruction Manual That Came With His New Sat-Nav System

The Fans' Guide To Football Grounds

The Highway Code

Is It Just Me Or Is Everything Sh*t?

Gangs by Ross Kemp

Hitler 1936 – 1945: Nemesis by Ian Kershaw

Nuts Magazine

Things To Be Found In Dads' Pockets

A penknife that the kids aren't allowed to touch.

A mobile phone which he has been instructed to use to contact Mum when one of the kids has a funny turn.

The phone number of NHS Direct in case Mum is unobtainable.

Some very small bits of broken toys that are clearly impossible to mend, but which he will attempt to fix anyway for reasons, variously, of parsimony, sentimentality and the primeval dad urge to try and put things back together even when the situation is clearly hopeless.

No paper money – that went years ago.

Large amounts of small change that Mum and the kids seem reluctant to use when they visit the shops. This means Dad's pockets bulge out as though he's had a hernia, his trousers weigh several kilograms and if he ever has to run anywhere the effect will be akin to a one-armed bandit that has suddenly decided to pay out.

A combination of cigarettes, nicotine gum and chewing gum that will be variously used depending on stress levels brought on by kids.

A bottle-opener (for emergencies).

Pictures of Mum and the kids (which he has been given and instructed to keep by Mum presumably as a means by which he can be identified if he ever tries to run away – not that he'll get far with all these things in his pockets and it will also, of course, be possible to locate him by following the trail of small change).

A selection of half-eaten sweets that the children got bored with, but which they promise him they will finish off later.

A list in Mum's handwriting of half a dozen errands he is expected to run while he's out.

A collection of acorns and leaves that his little kids have given him to look after while out on walks.

A selection of baby teeth he has been carrying around for a while, but which he keeps forgetting to get out and leave for the tooth fairy (which is a bit unfortunate as the kids are now all in their late teens).

Things Kids Can Get Away With That Dads Can't

Giving Mum a homemade card on her birthday.

Being forgiven for almost any misdemeanour by giving mum a big sloppy kiss.

Presenting Mum with a bunch of flowers freshly picked from her own front garden.

Bringing Mum a cold cup of tea and expecting her to be grateful.

Expecting a pat on the back for making the bed once a year.

Suddenly announcing that they've gone vegetarian and can't possibly eat dinner.

Ideal Dad versus Real Dad

Ideal dad	Real dad
Makes breakfast while mum has a lie-in	Makes a fuss if his own breakfast isn't all laid out ready for him when he gets up
Takes kids on exciting nature trails in country	Takes kids to pub and lets them play on broken swing in the pub garden
Is very careful to give them a balanced diet when Mum's away	Let's them eat all the same rubbish that he does
Is supportive of Mum in all aspects of childcare	Is himself, to all intents and purposes, the largest, most unruly and least helpful of Mum's kids
Teaches his children that it's not winning or losing that counts	Stands on the touchline swearing vociferously at the referee and attempting to pick arguments with parents of the opposing team
Tells them a story at bedtime and tucks them in	Tells Mum a story at bedtime and takes off to the pub
Helps them with homework so they get good grades	Is totally mystified by most of their homework because it's all completely changed since he was a lad... and what are grades anyway?

Boasting About Dad

Little Joshua is talking to a couple of boys in the school playground. Each is bragging about how fast their fathers are. The first one says, "My father runs the fastest. He can fire an arrow, start to run and get to the target before it hits!" The second one says, "You think that's fast? My father's a hunter. He can shoot his gun and be there before the bullet!" Joshua says, "You two know nothing about fast. My father's a civil servant. He stops working at five and he manages to get home by four thirty!"

Three boys were waiting for the bus. The first one says, "I have my grandma's eyes." The second says, "I have my mother's hair." "That's nothing," says the third. "I have my father's pants!"

Two small boys are boasting about their fathers and which is the most important. "Have you ever heard of the Suez Canal?" asks one boy. "Yes I have," says the other. "Well my dad's the guy who dug it," says the first boy. "That's nothing," says the second boy. "Have you heard of the Dead Sea?" "Yes," says the first. The second replies, "Well my dad's the guy who killed it."

Two boys are arguing about who's dad was richer. The first says, "My dad is so rich he's going to buy the Pacific Ocean." "Oh yeah," says the second. "Well, if you don't shut up, I'll tell my dad not to sell it."

Two kids are arguing over whose father is the biggest scaredy-cat. The first kid says, "My dad is so scared that when lightning strikes, he hides underneath the bed." The second kid replies, "Yeah? Well, that's nothing. My dad is so scared that when my mum has to work the nightshift, he sleeps with the lady next door."

That's My Boy! (Ways In Which Boys Can Make Dad Proud)

When driving his pedal car he shouts at other pavement users when they do anything wrong.

When playing "Mummies and Daddies" he refuses to cook because it's "women's work".

His alphabet training begins, "A is for 'apple', B is for 'beer'..."

When the local MP visited his school and asked his name he cited the Data Protection Act.

When girls ask him to play kiss chase he gets them to sign a pre-nuptial agreement.

You Know You've Hired The Wrong Entertainer For Your Children's Party When...

All the balloon animals are ribbed and lubricated.

He asks you to sign an insurance disclaimer before he'll start.

He demands payment up front in cash in a plain brown envelope.

He does that "smashing the child's watch with a hammer" trick, but fails to take it off the child's wrist first.

He stops for a cigarette break every 15 minutes.

He's dropped off at your house by a prison guard who says he'll collect him in two hours.

His calling card has a "parental advisory" sticker on it.

His first party game is a yard of ale contest.

His second one is mud wrestling.

His ventriloquist dummy is dressed in a Nazi uniform.

The music he uses for musical chairs is Gary Glitter's *Greatest Hits*.

Dad Knows Best

A father and his son are out fishing one day. "Dad," says the little boy, "why do boats float?" "Ooh! I don't know that," replies Dad. "How do fish breath underwater, Dad?" asks the boy, "Nope. Don't know that either," replies Dad. "Dad," says the boy. "Why is the sky blue?" "Er... no. I've no idea," replies Dad. A few moments pass then the boy says, "Dad, you don't mind me asking you all these questions do you?" "Of course not," says Dad. "If you don't ask questions how are you ever going to learn anything?"

> **"I want to share something with you: the three little sentences that will get you through life. Number 1: Cover for me. Number 2: Oh, good idea, Boss! Number 3: It was like that when I got here."**
> **Homer Simpson**

A daddy mouse and a little baby mouse are walking along, when all of a sudden, a cat attacks them. The daddy mouse goes, "BARK!" and the cat runs away. "You see, son," says the daddy mouse. "Now do you understand why it's important to learn a foreign language?"

> **Son, if you really want something in this life, you have to work for it. Now be quiet! They're about to announce the lottery numbers.**
> **Homer Simpson**

"Lisa, if you don't like your job you don't strike. You just go in every day and do it really half-assed. That's the American way."
Homer Simpson

"Dad always thought laughter was the best medicine, which I guess is why several of us died of tuberculosis."
Jack Handy

A four-year-old boy is eating an apple in the back of the car, when he asks, "Daddy, why is my apple starting to turn brown?" "Ah!" says Dad. "That's because the skin of the apple exists to protect the flesh inside. After you ate the skin from the apple, the flesh came into contact with the air, that caused it to oxidize and the resulting chemical reaction changed the molecular structure turning the apple flesh a different colour." A long silence followed before the little boy asked quietly, "Daddy, are you talking to me?"

"I have always had the feeling I could do anything and my dad told me I could. I was in college before I found out he might be wrong."
Ann Richards

"If something's hard to do, then it's not worth doing."
Homer Simpson

In the USA a little boy's dad was constantly telling him, "You know, son, when Abraham Lincoln was your age, he had a job. When Abraham Lincoln was your age, he walked 12 miles to get to school." In the end the boy got fed up with this and snapped back with, "Dad, when Abraham Lincoln was your age, he was already President, so just shut up! OK!"

Kids, you tried your best and you failed miserably. The lesson is, never try.
Homer Simpson

One day Dad gets fed up with his young son asking questions all the time. "You're always asking questions," says Dad. "I'd like to know what would have happened if I'd asked as many questions when I was little." "Well," says the boy, "perhaps then you'd have been able to answer some of mine today."

Things Dads Don't Ever Need to Worry About Buying For Themselves

Socks, underpants etc.
When Dad was a little boy his birthday and Christmas were the most exciting times of the year. Little Dad would scarcely be able to sleep the night before these illustrious days. Instead he would lie awake in a state of feverish excitement awaiting the arrival of hordes of football, Action Man, Thunderbirds, James Bond, Star Wars or pop music related gifts. Now that Dad is a dad, he instead looks forward to Christmas and birthdays in their new guise as the days on which his underwear and sock drawers will be extensively restocked and on which friends and family get to see exactly what he will be wearing under his trousers during the coming months. For some reason Dad now has no problem whatsoever sleeping prior to his birthday or Christmas.

Mobile phones
Dads will often choose to avoid buying mobile phones for themselves. Dad's unwillingness to spend any more money than is strictly necessary will instead result in him obtaining his mobile via the hand-me-down system. This system traditionally used to go down the age groups with the youngest child ending up with well-worn items from his elders and betters. Now that Dad is a dad the system seems to have

gone into complete reverse and should more accurately be known as the hand-me-up system. It means that Dad's mobile phone will be one that was once bought at enormous expense for his son or daughter, but which they now refuse to be seen dead with. This explains why when Dad's mobile rings it will play a melody from an old McFly single. When Dad whips it out of his pocket, the phone will prove to be a model that is three years out-of-date, pink and decorated with the legend "Hello Kitty".

Portraits of themselves

Not for Dad the expense of commissioning a picture of himself from some overpaid portrait painter. Instead his distinctive physiognomy will provide near constant inspiration to the creative impulses of junior members of his family. He will have drawers stuffed full to bursting with impressionistic studies of himself done in watercolours or crayon. These will include a number of pictures of a man with three hairs arranged equidistantly around the top of his head, eyes that appear to be attempting to look at each other and a nose almost as big as his skull. The composition will be labelled for all to see as "Daddy". In a number of these pictures "Daddy" will be depicted in a state of extreme bad temper possibly alongside a piece of self-assembly furniture. In such "still life with Ikea corner unit" studies, "Daddy" will have a word balloon next to him which conveys his language by means of hieroglyphics, including asterisks, swirly lines, exclamation marks and skulls.

Pens

For similar reasons to his reliance on an out-of-date, bright pink mobile phone, Dad will possess an extensive collection of day-glo-style pens that he is forever trying to get a bit more use out of before they are consigned to the bin. Thus, whenever Dad has to sign his name or fill in an official form, his handwriting will appear in bright green, pink, purple, gold or silver ink, possibly imbued with a shiny metallic effect.

Coffee cream chocolates

Occasionally Dad may be offered a large exciting looking box
that apparently contains a great selection of fine chocolates.
Unfortunately when Dad peers inside this massive container
of mouth-watering sweetmeats, there will be little left to greet
him. He will most likely find two sad, solitary, coffee flavoured
survivors huddling together in one corner following an all day
purge on their fellows inflicted by Mum and the kids. These
foul tasting, Nescafe-topped excuses for chocolates would
once have been thrown to the family dog. These days more
people are aware that chocolate is poisonous to dogs, so they
are discarded via the household's alternative walking waste
disposal system: Dad.

That's My Girl!
(Ways In Which Girls Can Make Dad Proud)

When driving her pedal car she refuses to be intimidated by little
boys in their pedal cars.

When playing "Mummies and Daddies" she refuses to cook
because she doesn't want to be a stereotypical female.

Her alphabet training begins, "A is for 'apple', B is for 'Behave
yourself!'"

When the local MP visited and asked her name she said, "You
can call me madam."

When boys want to play kiss chase she makes them buy her
dinner first.

Dads' Main Enemies In Life

Teachers – they give him far too much homework.

Nutritionists – what exactly is the problem with giving babies a couple of beers and a bowl of Doritos for breakfast?

Milkmen – you've eventually got the baby sleeping soundly when "clink clink," Ernie arrives and wakes you all up again!

Child experts – what do they know? They should all be made to live with my kids for a week – they'd soon change their tune.

Single mates – coming round here with their talk of nights out at the pub, chatting up women, golf weekends, all-night parties, football trips to Belgium. They seem so immature. It just makes you so… jealous.

The wife – whoever said marriage is a partnership was lying. It's like World War Three – with nappies.

Children – every sentence they come out with seems to begin with the phrase "But Mummy says…"

Younger dads – however old you are there's always some younger dad who never seems to run out of energy playing with his kids, beats you in the parents' race at sports day and still has more hair than you!

Health visitors – they come round to check on the baby's health (supposedly) and are really spying on how much you drink and smoke, and whether you can actually be trusted with a baby.

In-laws – yes, the mother-in-law is the ultimate clichéd hate figure, but maybe it's for a reason. You could be Brad Pitt, the Pope and Cliff Richard all rolled into one, but you'd never be good enough for her daughter, oh no, and even your father-in-law thinks you're a slob who drives too fast, drinks too much and is a bad example to the children. Perhaps he thinks you're a bit too much like him for comfort.

Other mums – you may take the children to school, cook their tea when they get home, take them to the park at weekends and you may even, in extreme circumstances, sew their nametags into their school uniforms and bake your own cakes, but you can never be accepted as an equal by mums – you're one of the enemy, mate!

Cooking – Dad Style

God bless the microwave – Dad's the man who put the "ping!" into shopping.

Either Dad's on a health kick or he's realized that salad doesn't need to be cooked.

The neighbours always know when we're having chips for tea because the fire brigade turn up.

Dad's speciality is a delicious, succulent burger in a lightly toasted bun with relish and skinny chips – unfortunately he can't afford to take the family out to a fast-food restaurant every night.

Dad loves barbecuing, because however much he cremates the food it will never set off the smoke alarm.

Dad likes to create a bit of variety with even the most ordinary of dishes, so beans on toast becomes: beans on floor, beans on fire, beans on baby's head...

Dad's a bit mystified by some of the ingredients Mum uses so he doesn't go near them – in fact he's a bit worried that she's so fond of them she's started giving them pet names like Basil and Rosemary (weird or what?)

But there's one magic ingredient that never fails – tomato ketchup. However burnt those sausages, however bland that pasta, however yucky that cabbage, good ol' ketchup can save the day, but even the kids object when he puts it on the porridge – even if it is burnt.

But Dad is good at preparation. Before he starts on a meal he always makes sure everything is ready and in place – ingredients, cooking pots, fire blanket, extinguisher, air freshener...

Some meals are a bit complicated for a man of Dad's cooking ability, so he's invented his own simplified versions: Chilli non carne, Toad, Beef tomato Wellington, Seize-a-salad, Ploughman's skipped lunch, Kentucky fried chicken supreme... Life's just too short isn't it, Dad?

Things You'll Never Hear A Dad Say

I've had a quiet day at work, why don't you let me look after the baby while you have a night out with the girls?

Hey, that's a fun idea – using my electric drill because the food mixer broke!

It's OK, I can watch the cup final highlights on the news later kids. Just carry on watching *CITV* for as long as you want.

Put that vacuum cleaner down this minute and let me have a go for a change!

That bubblegum on the car seats is quite good in a way, because it stops me sliding around while I'm driving.

Come home whatever time you like – you're only 14 once!

I bet my old mates in the darts team secretly envy me being able to stay home with my family every Friday night now.

You're absolutely right, dear, I am driving too fast.

It's about time your pocket money was raised young man!

You may not want to watch *Teletubbies*, but I do, OK?

Damn the expense, our daughter is only getting married once!

Sorry, son, I'm far too old to have a go at your Wii boxing game.

Now, young lady, you go out and have a great time and phone me when you're ready to be picked up – at any time of the night.

You're pregnant? Well, congratulations, love, but try not to let it affect your GCSEs.

No son of mine is going to become a football club owner!

Hey, let's save Mum from cooking tonight and go out for a nice expensive meal.

You Might Be A Dad Who Sets A Bad Example If ...

You have an ashtray fitted to the side of the cot to get you through the bedtime story.

The first card game you teach the kids is stud poker.

The kids learn their first swear words by watching you attempt to put together a self-assembly wardrobe.

You continually tell them how much nicer their Barbie dolls look compared to Mum who, "has really let herself go since you came along".

Rather than traditional nursery rhymes, you teach them gangsta rap lyrics.

Rather than building with plastic bricks, you provide your children with a seemingly limitless supply of empty beer cans to use instead.

You not only buy them toy guns, but toy silencers and dum-dum bullets too.

You amuse the children every evening before bedtime by tattooing yourself in front of them.

As soon as they are born, you put their names down to join the local street gang.

You buy them real cigarettes – sweet ones are bad for their teeth.

You're a life member of the AA and you don't even drive.

You beat them at "scissors, paper, stone" by introducing a nuclear device.

You make the local Godfather their godfather.

You teach them spelling by making them read your tattoos.

When they ask for a kitten you insist on getting them a pit bull terrier.

The Most Annoying Things Dads Do

You ruffle the kids' hair whenever you say hello, goodbye or tell them they're "a little monkey".

Come on, Dad! Just because your hair's beginning to go AWOL doesn't mean you need to try and get the kids started with a bald patch as well by rubbing their little heads until smoke begins to rise.

You try to get the kids interested in all your boring hobbies.

Sorry, Dad! The tiny tots simply are not interested in your extensive (though doubtless fascinating) collection of turpentine and other wood preservatives from around the world.

You suggest playing football just so you can show off.

Shame on you, Dad! After all these years the only people you've ever been able to find who are worse at football than you, are the ones who only learnt to walk last Wednesday.

You buy the children a new gadget and then won't let them near it for the first half hour.

OK, you might let them have a little go if they promise to show you how it works.

When the kids bring home their first boyfriend/girlfriend you refuse to leave the front room.

But of course! You remember all too clearly what you were like when you were their age. So you're hardly going to let them get up to any of the things you used to get up to. It would be a disaster wouldn't it? They might eventually end up like you!

When they bring home their second boyfriend/girlfriend you get mixed up and call them by the name of the first one.

This appalling behaviour will in fact continue indefinitely. So by the time your offspring brings home their 20th boyfriend/ girlfriend, you will be able to treat the new partner to a Top of the Pops *style rundown of all their predecessors. Well done, Dad!*

You moan to the kids about Mum.

Surely nothing can go wrong with this carefully thought out plan of action can it, Dad? After all, Mum's never going to find out what you said about her, is she?

Crap Jokes That Dads All Over The World Don't Seem To Be Able To Stop Themselves From Making

If Dad sees a stuffed animal head mounted on a wall, he will say, "Wow! That creature must have been going pretty fast when it hit that wall!"

CRAP JOKES THAT DADS ALL OVER THE WORLD...

If you say, "I'm off," Dad will reply, "Are you? I wondered what the smell was."

If you're out in the car and ask, "Where are we?" Dad will respond, "In the car."

If you've been struggling to do something for a little while, Dad will come and ask you, "Can I give you a hand?" If you say yes, Dad will start a slow handclap.

When Dad finds himself behind a slow hesitant driver, he will cry, "Come on!! What are you waiting for? Christmas?"

When Dad is driving past a cemetery he will tell you, "You know they put the fence up to keep everyone in!"

When Dad is driving past a cemetery he will also tell you, "You know that's the dead centre of town!"

When Dad is driving past a cemetery he will further tell you, "You know that place is pretty popular. People are dying to get in there!"

When driving past a herd of black and white cows Dad will say, "Oooh, it must be cold out there. Look at those cows. They're Friesian!"

When driving past a woman Dad will say, "Marks out of ten? Yes, I'd definitely give her one!"

When passing a neighbour who is washing their car Dad will say to them, "You can do mine next, if you want!"

When the phone rings Dad will tell you, "If that's for me, don't answer it."

While on a day out, if he sees an information sign that says something like, "The rocks in this area are 50 million years old..." Dad will inevitably start to sing "Happy Birthday to you, Happy Birthday to you..."

If you say, "Dad, I'm hungry," he will reply, "Hello, Hungry. I'm Dad."

When eating at a restaurant Dad will amusingly try to order "soup in a basket".

When dining out with Dad, if someone drops a plate, he will cry, "It wasn't me!"

When dining out with Dad, if someone drops a plate, he will say, "Sack the juggler!"

When dining out with Dad, if someone drops a plate, he will shout, "Taxi!"

When a waiter says, "I'll be your waiter tonight," Dad will respond with the line, "And I'll be your customer!"

If he takes you out to a Greek restaurant, Dad will look at the menu and ask the waiter, "Could you recommend something. It's all Greek to me."

If at the end of the meal Dad is offered a hot towel, he will say, "No, thank you. I'm full!"

At dinnertime, after you've helped yourself to gravy, Dad will say, "Do you want some food to go with your gravy?"

After a large meal Dad will inevitably declare, "Well that was nice. So what's for dinner?"

Immediately after a large meal Dad will say, "Oooh! It's a good thing we ate when we did, because do you know what? I'm not a bit hungry now!"

When you say to Dad, "Please may I leave the table?" he will reply, "OK, but where are you going to leave it?"

Just before going to the bathroom Dad will tell you to "give the sewage plant a call and let them know there's a large one on the way!"

When Dad is about to fart he will invite you to, "Pull my finger!"

After farting Dad will say, "Ooops! I think I've had a slippage."

After farting Dad will say, "Oooh! Better out than in."

After farting Dad will say, "Speak up, Mr Brown. You're through."

After farting Dad will say, "Phew! I'm glad I'm not downwind of that one."

Embarrassing Dads

"It is a wise child that knows its own father and an unusual one that unreservedly approves of him."

Mark Twain

"My boy, you took the words right out of my mouth. I'm ashamed to be your father. You're a disgrace to our family name of Wagstaff, if such a thing is possible."

Groucho Marx

"I remember the difficulty in Glasgow of my father being a teetotaller – and the shame on Saturday nights of him being constantly thrown into pubs."

Arnold Brown

"I remember the shouts of "SCAB!" as my father went to work. "SCAB!" they would shout during the great dermatologists' strike..."

Harry Hill

"My dad was the town drunk. Most of the time that's not so bad – but New York City?"

Henny Youngman

"My dad was too proud to beg on the streets – so he used to beg indoors."

Ronnie Corbett

"A lot of controversy over this possible invasion of Iraq. In fact, Nelson Mandela was so upset, he called Bush's dad. How embarrassing, when world leaders start calling your father."

Jay Leno

"I never got along with my dad. Kids used to come up to me and say, 'My dad can beat up your dad.' I'd say, 'Yeah? When?'"

Bill Hicks

Helping With The Housework

Two dads are talking. "You know what my fantasy is?" says the first. "To have two women at the same time." "Yeah, that's mine too," says the second, "But only if one of them is cooking and the other is cleaning."

Mum can't understand Dad's methods of doing the housework. When he notices a bit of fluff on the carpet that the vacuum cleaner has gone over, but hasn't picked up, he bends down, picks it up, looks at it closely, but doesn't put it in the bin. Instead he puts it back down on the floor and sees if the vacuum cleaner will pick it up on the second attempt.

"The trouble with me lad, is I'm too easy bloody going. She walks all over me. I mean, the day she does work in the bakery; it can be half seven, or a quarter to eight before my tea's ready. But I don't say nothing, I just get on with it."

Jim Royle/*The Royle Family*

Mum asks Dad, "So, when are you going to think about mowing the lawn?" "Straight after I've thought about painting the shed," says Dad.

Dad has too many things on his mind. This morning he had an accident whilst boiling an egg. He held the egg in his hand and plopped his watch into the pan of boiling water.

Dad says to his little boy, "I can't believe the colour of you. How do you manage to get so filthy all the time? Look at me. I manage to stay clean." "Well," says the boy, "I'm a lot closer to the ground than you are."

An old man complains to Dad one night in the pub. "My wife is a terribly lazy woman," says the old man. "She never does any housework." "Oh yes," says Dad. "Yes," says the old man. "Every time I go to wee in the kitchen sink, it's full of dirty dishes."

A little boy calls to his father, "Daddy, Daddy, please can I have another glass of water?" "Oh, son," says the dad, "I've run up and down the stairs with ten glasses of water for you already!" "I know that," says the boy, "but my bedroom's still on fire!"

The Kids Are Doing Dad Proud At School

Once a year Dad is sent a school report and from that is supposed to glean everything he needs to know about his child's progress – or lack of it.

But although little Jimmy has a D in science he can download enough info from the Internet to help him bluff his way through his homework in 30 seconds flat. And although little Daisy has the flimsiest grasp of mathematics she can work out her daily calorie intake, optimum weight and required supermodel dimensions to three decimal places without the aid of an electronic calculator.

And what about all that other stuff they learn which isn't even on the curriculum? Has anyone ever taught a child how to send a text, solve a Rubik cube or annoy their dad when he's trying to read the flipping paper? Of course not – they're picked up by some sort of cultural osmosis, and that's what kids are really learning at school. That, and how to speak English as a second language: the first being "Kiddish". They learn how to swear, how to impersonate teachers, tell jokes, misbehave on the bus, smoke without anyone seeing, get round the school dress code, and a million and one other things.

And if you're lucky they may just pick up what you would call some "proper knowledge" too.

School – it's an education innit?

At the beginning of the school year, a primary school teacher is getting to know her new pupils. She goes round the class asking them all what their mummies and daddies do. Finally she comes to one little girl and asks her, "And what about you? What does your daddy do?" And the little girl replies, "Whatever Mummy tells him."

One morning the receptionist at little Johnny's school gets a call. "I'm very sorry," says a strange voice at the end of the phone. "But little Johnny isn't feeling very well so he won't be coming into school today." "OK," says the receptionist. "And who's that speaking?" The voice replies, "This is my dad."

Dad takes his son into a prospective school. He asks the head teacher, "So do you get good SATs results here?" We certainly do," says the head teacher. "We guarantee satisfaction… or we return the student."

A little boy gets home from his first day at school. "What was the first thing you learned?" asks Dad. "How to talk without moving my lips," says the boy.

A little boy gets home from his first day at school. "How did it go, son?" asks Dad. "It was fine," says the boy. "Except for some old woman we had to call 'teacher' who kept spoiling our fun."

A little boy has just started school. Dad asks him, "So, son, how are you enjoying going to school?" "The going bit and the coming home bit are OK," says the boy. "It's just the in between bit I'm not so keen on."

A little boy comes home from school one day and tells his mum and dad, "I'm really glad you named me Tommy." "Oh yes," say his parents. "And why's that?" "Because," says the boy, "that's what everyone at school calls me."

Dad asks his little boy, "What did you learn in school today?" "Not enough," says the boy. "I've got to go back again tomorrow!"

Dad says to his daughter, "So did you learn anything at school today?" "Yes," says the little girl proudly. "I learnt how to write." "Wow," says Dad. "So what did you write?" "I don't know," she says. "We don't get taught to read until next week."

Dad says to his son, "Where's the money I just gave you?" "I just swallowed it," says the boy. "Why did you do that, son?" asks Dad. "You said it was my lunch money," replies the boy.

Dad's little boy is still in bed at eight thirty in the morning. "Hurry up, son," says Dad. "You'll be late for school." "But I'm not well," says the boy. "Oh yes," says Dad. "And where exactly is it you don't feel well?" "In school," says the boy.

A small boy is dawdling along to school. "Hurry up son! You'll be late!" shouts his father out of the window. "There's no rush," the boy calls back. "They're open till three thirty this afternoon."

How is education supposed to make me feel smarter? Besides, every time I learn something new, it pushes some old stuff out of my brain. Remember when I took that home wine making course and I forgot how to drive?
Homer Simpson

Dad collars his little boy one day and says sternly, "I hear you skipped school yesterday to play football." "That's a damn lie," says the boy. "And what's more I've got the fish to prove it."

Dad grabs hold of his youngest son and says crossly, "I've just had a letter from the head teacher at your school. It seems he's rather concerned about your appearance." "What's the matter with it?" asks the boy. "Well," says Dad, "apparently you haven't made one since last term!"

After a day off from school, Dad's little boy hands in a note to the teacher to explain his absence. "But," says the teacher, "this note from your father looks like it was written by you." "Yes," says the boy, "that's because he had to borrow my pen to write it."

A teacher noticed that one of the boys in her class was making faces at another boy. She told him to stop it at once and said, "When I was a little girl I was told that if I made horrible faces and the wind changed my face would stay like that." The boy looked at her for a moment and said, "Well then, Miss, you can't say you weren't warned."

Dad says to his little boy, "Did you miss school yesterday." "Yes," says the boy," but not very much."

On the way to lunch, a teacher spotted two boys playfully fighting near the front of the queue. She asked one of the boys to go to the back of the line and he came straight back to the front again. "Why didn't you wait at the end of the line?" asked the teacher. The boy replied, "I couldn't. Someone was already there."

At the end of a test at school the teacher has a quiet word with Dad's son. "I think you've copied your answers off the little girl sitting next to you." "That's a lie," says Dad's little boy. "What makes you think that?" "To all the questions where she's written 'I don't know,'" says the teacher, "you've answered, 'Neither do I.'"

During a test at school, teacher tells Dad's little boy, "I hope I didn't just see you looking at your neighbour's paper." "I hope you didn't see me either!" says the boy.

> **I have never been jealous. Not even when my dad finished fifth grade a year before I did.**
> Jeff Foxworthy

Little Benjamin's public school raises its fees, but sends out letters mistakenly saying that the new fees need to be paid "per anum" rather than the correct "per annum". Benjamin's dad indignantly writes back to say that he agrees to the new fees, but would rather continue paying through the nose if that's quite all right.

Nicholas was a very intelligent little boy from a humble background and his parents managed to get him into a good school, so by now he had a far better command of English than they did. One day he came home and said, "Father, may

I relate to you a narrative?" "What's a narrative when it's at home, Nicholas?" his dad asked. "A narrative, Father," explained Nicholas, "is a tale." "Oh, I see," said his father, and so Nicholas told him his story. That evening just as he was about to go to bed he said, "Shall I extinguish the light, Father?" "What's extinguish?" his dad asked. "Extinguish means 'to put out', Father," said the boy. "Oh, right, OK, son, go on then." The next day, a rather posh neighbour came to tea and the family dog began to make a nuisance of himself by begging for scraps from the table. "Nicholas," said his dad, trying to impress the neighbour, "take that dog by the narrative and extinguish him!"

Matthew came home from school and said "Dad, our English teacher set us some work today. She said we had to describe ourselves in ten words or less. I wrote, 'Succinct.'"

Mum and Dad send their dim son to a tutor to help him catch up on his schoolwork. After a month they ask for a progress report and are told, "He's getting straight As." "That's fantastic," say the parents. "Yes, they're great," says the tutor, "but his Bs are still a little wonky."

In The Classroom

The teacher asks Dad's youngest, "Why is it that you're never able to answer any of the questions I ask you?" "If I could," says the boy, "there wouldn't be much point in me coming here, would there!"

The English teacher notices Eddie staring out of the window and calls out a question, "You boy! Give me two pronouns!" The boy looks round and says, "Who? Me?"

The farmer's son didn't go to school one day. The following day, when the teacher asked him why he had been absent, the boy said, "Our cow was on heat, so I had to take her to the bull." "That's all very well," said the teacher, "but I don't see why your father couldn't have done that." "Oh he couldn't have, Miss," said the little boy. "It has to be the bull."

The teacher asks her class, "OK, class, which do you think is more important, the sun or the moon?" Little George puts his hand up and says, "The moon!" "That's interesting," says the teacher. "Why do you think that?" "Because," says George, "the moon gives us light at night when it's dark and we need it, but the sun only gives us light during the day when it's bright enough already."

The teacher asks his class, "When was Rome built?" A hand goes up and a boy says, "I think it was at night, sir." "What do you mean 'at night'?" asks the teacher. "Well," says the boy, "my dad always says that Rome wasn't built in a day."

The teacher asks his class, "Who can tell me how many seconds there are in a year?" "There's 12, sir," says one boy. "Twelve?" says the teacher. "How do you work that out?" "Well," says the boy, "there's the second of January, the second of February, the second of March…"

The teacher asks little Billy to go up to the map in front of the class and show everyone where America is. As Billy does this the teacher says, "Very good. Now, what was the name of the person who discovered America?" "Billy!" shout the children in unison.

The teacher tells Dad's little boy, "You know, your handwriting really is atrocious. Why don't you try to write more neatly?" "Because," says the boy, "then you'd realize I can't spell."

The teacher asks little Tommy to think of a sentence beginning with the word "I". Tommy starts off, "I is…" "Oh no, Tommy," says the teacher. "That's wrong straightaway isn't it? You must say 'I am' rather than 'I is'." "OK," says Tommy. "I am the ninth letter of the alphabet."

The teacher says to little Georgie, "You've only drawn a cow. I thought I asked you to draw a picture of a cow eating some hay earlier on." "Well," says George, "that was so long ago, the cow's eaten all the hay."

The teacher tells his class they have 45 minutes to write an essay on the subject of cricket. A minute or so later, little Tommy hands in his paper. "How have you managed to finish so quickly?" asks the teacher. "Let's hear what you wrote." Tommy clears his throat and reads out his essay: "Match called off because of rain."

The teacher tells the class, "I'm going to ask you a really easy question now, so I want you to answer altogether. So, what is two times two?" "Altogether!" shouts the class.

Dad's young son is doing a class in food technology at school. One day the teacher asks him to name the four main food groups. The little boy thinks for a moment then says, "Is it frozen, instant, canned and lite?"

The teacher was testing her pupils on their knowledge of opposites. "James," she says. "What is the opposite of joy?" "Sadness," says James. "Very good," says the teacher. "And Colleen, what is the opposite of depression?" "Elation, Miss?" says Colleen. "Very good, Colleen," says the teacher. "And Patrick, how about the opposite of woe?" "Is it 'Giddy up,' Miss?" asks Patrick.

Young Joe was having a lot of difficulty learning French at school. To encourage him, his teacher said, "Never mind Joe, just keep at it. You'll know you're beginning to get somewhere when you start dreaming in French." A few weeks later Joe rushed into his French class all excited. "Miss! I had a dream last night and everyone was speaking in French!" "Fantastic!" said the teacher. "What were they saying?" "I don't know," said Joe, "I couldn't understand a word of it."

During a nature study period at school, the teacher points to Dad's son and asks him, "What do we call the outside layer of a tree?" Dad's son looks blank so the teacher tells him, "Bark, boy! Bark!" "Woof, woof, woof!" cries Dad's little boy.

In a grammar lesson Mrs Jones said, "Paul, give me a sentence with a direct object." Paul replied, "Everyone thinks you are the best teacher in the school." "Thank you, Paul," responded Mrs Jones. "But what is the object?" "To get the best mark possible," said Paul.

A teacher asked her primary school class to make up sentences using the words: defeat, detail and defence. There was a pause before young Marlon raised his hand and said he could make a sentence with them: "The cow jumped over defence and detail went over defeat."

IN THE CLASSROOM

In a maths lesson, the teacher asks Dad's little boy, "Tell me, if you add 84 and 26 then divide the total by four, what will you get?" "The wrong answer," says Dad's son.

Dad's little boy goes to his teacher at school and says, "I ain't got no crayons, Miss." "What do you mean 'I ain't got no crayons'?" asks the teacher. "Let me demonstrate. I don't have any crayons. You don't have any crayons. We don't have any crayons. They don't have any crayons. Do you see?" "I think so," says the little boy. "So why ain't no-one got no crayons round here?"

A group of young children are sitting in a circle with their teacher learning about animal sounds. She goes round each child in turn asking them questions. "Now then, Davy," says the teacher, "what noise does a cow make?" "It goes 'moo', Miss," answers Davy. "Very good," says the teacher. "Alice, what noise does a cat make?" "It goes 'miaow', Miss," answers Alice. "Excellent, Alice," says the teacher. "Now, Jamie, do you know what sound a lamb makes?" "Yes, Miss," says Jamie. "It goes 'baa'." "Very good indeed," says the teacher. "And finally, Lucy, what sound does a mouse make?" "Please, Miss," says Lucy. "Does it go 'click'?"

A primary school teacher asks a little boy if he knows his numbers. "Yes I do," says the little boy. "My father taught me." "Good. Then tell me what comes after three," asks the teacher. "Four," says the boy. "Very good," says the teacher. "And what comes after six?" "Seven," says the boy. "Excellent," says the teacher. "Your dad has obviously taught you very well. But do you know what comes after ten?" "I certainly do," says the little boy. "It's a jack!"

137

A teacher said to one of her pupils, "Billy, if both of your parents had been born in 1967, how old would they be now?" After a few moments, Billy answered, "It depends." "It depends on what?" she asked. "It depends on whether you ask my father or my mother."

After the school holidays the new teacher was asking her primary class what they'd been doing during the summer. "What did you do then, Mitzi?" the teacher asked one of the little girls. "We went to the seaside, Miss," said Mitzi. "That sounds nice," said the teacher. "And what about you, Polly? What did you do in the holidays?" "My mum and dad took me out on lots of bike rides," said the little girl. "Wow! That sounds like fun!" said the teacher. She carried on asking the rest of the children until she got to Jamie, who was sitting quietly at the back. "And what did you do in the summer, Jamie?" she asked. "Nothing," said Jamie shyly. "Did you do anything with your family?" the teacher asked. "Did you go anywhere?" "Yes," said Jamie. "Did you go to the seaside?" "No!" said the boy. "Did you ride bikes?" "No, definitely not!" said Jamie indignantly, "We can never ride bikes together!" "Why ever not?" asked the teacher. "I don't know," said Jamie. "But my dad always said that when my mum and my sister start 'cycling' together things are going to be really bad."

A teacher was explaining to her class of ten-year-olds one day what an abstract noun was. She said, "It's something you can think of, but you can't touch. Can anyone give me an example of one?" "Yes," said young Damien. "My dad's new car."

One day in class the teacher asks, "Simon, if I had seven oranges in my right hand and 11 oranges in my left hand, what would I have?" "Huge hands, sir," says Simon.

A primary school teacher was overseeing her pupils as they experimented with their computers. One boy sat staring at the screen, unsure how to get the machine going. The teacher walked over and read what was on his screen. In her most reassuring voice, she said, "The computer wants to know what your name is." After she walked away, the boy leaned toward the screen and whispered, "My name is David."

The teacher asks her class, "Now, can anybody give any examples of a coincidence?" "I can, Miss," says Little Jimmy. "My mum and dad got engaged on the same day, married on the same day and not only that, it was at exactly the same time."

Teacher asks her class for a sentence with the word "beautiful" in it twice. First, she asks Daisy, who responds, "My dad bought my mum a beautiful dress and she looked very beautiful in it." "Well done, Daisy," says the teacher. She then asks Joseph to think of an example. "My mummy planned a beautiful birthday party and it turned out beautifully," he says. "Excellent, Joseph," says the teacher. Next up is Liam who says, "Last night my sister told my dad that she was pregnant, and he said, 'Beautiful! Flipping beautiful!'"

Things Dads Learn At School

A detailed knowledge of every 4x4 currently on the market.

Female teachers will automatically assume that you're second in command in the family.

If you pick the kids up from school it either means you're:

Unemployed and useless
A bit of a weirdo
Trying to check out the other mums
To be treated with extreme caution
In a same-sex relationship and must have adopted your kids

If a woman says, "Ah! Are you feeling strong?" immediately clutch your heart and let out a little groan.

It is more difficult to find a parking space outside a school than it is outside Harrods on the first day of their sale.

Never volunteer for anything, as you will end up doing it for the next five years.

Being a man you're expected to be useless, so if you actually remember to bring in your child's swimming things on the right day you're regarded as something approaching a genius by the other mums.

Whatever you did or how you did it when you were at school is now totally irrelevant and of no practical use when trying to help your child today.

Even if your children respect their teachers the final arbiter in any quest for knowledge is the eminent Professor Google.

The nativity play is now an excuse for parents to show off who has the best digital camera.

Never complain at parents' evening that your child is slipping behind as the teacher will suggest you do more work with them at home.

Dad Helps With The Homework

A young teacher is handing out marked homework books to her pupils. The previous night's homework had been to define a list of words. She calls little Callum over to her desk. "You did very well, Callum," he says. "You defined all the words correctly apart from one. For 'bachelor', you've written 'blissfully happy man'. You should have written that a bachelor is an unmarried man." "Should I?" replies Callum. "I'd better tell Dad, he was helping me with my homework last night."

Little Benjamin was doing his geography homework one evening when he turned to his father and said, "Dad, where would I find the Andes?" "Don't ask me," said his father. "Ask your mother. She puts everything away in this house."

The teacher thinks little Johnny has been cheating on his homework. "Did your dad help you do some of your homework last night?" "No! That's not true at all," says Johnny. "He did all of it."

A little boy tells his dad, "I've got to go out and play with my friends. Could you do my homework for me while I'm gone?" "No!" says his dad. "It just wouldn't be right, would it?" "Well, no, probably not," says the boy. "But you could at least have a go couldn't you?"

A primary school teacher decides to poll the class on the difficulty of the previous night's homework. She asks, "How many pupils were able to complete the assignment *without* their parents' help?" About 25 per cent of the class raise their hands. "How many pupils were able to complete the assignment *with* the help of a parent?" About 70 per cent of the class raise their hands. The teacher notices about 5 per cent of the class still have not answered. She then calls out, "How many pupils had to help a parent complete the assignment?"

Dad gets young Wayne to read out the answer he wrote down for his homework. "Lkjgncdho kjjknff uui ghwqanxzl imlkh thxxxzkqqq ogrhew fffahhg jkolm mnmko purp," reads Wayne. "That's absolute nonsense isn't it?" says Dad. "I know," says Wayne. "But the teacher said to answer in my own words."

Dad is helping his son with his homework and is trying to explain addition. "George, if I laid two eggs over there and two eggs over here, how many would I have?" "I don't know," says little George. "Let's see you do it first."

When Dad came home from work one day he was amazed to see his son Alex sitting on the family dog's back, writing in a book. "What are you doing!?" he asked incredulously. "Well, my teacher told us to write a story on our favourite animal. So that's why I'm sitting here and why Lucy's sitting in the fish pond!"

Little Johnny asks his dad for help with the homework he's been given for his English class. "Dad, do you know what the difference is between the words 'potential' and 'reality'?" "It's difficult to put into words, son," says Dad, "but I can demonstrate what the difference is to you. Go and ask your mother if she would sleep with Robert Redford for a million pounds. Then go and ask your sister if she would sleep with Brad Pitt for a million pounds. Then come back here and tell me what you've learnt." Little Johnny is puzzled, but decides to go along with it. He asks his mother, "Mum, if someone gave you a million pounds, would you sleep with Robert Redford?" His mother looks around shyly and then with a little smile on her face says, "Don't tell your father, but yes! Yes, I would." Next Johnny goes to his sister and asks her, "If someone gave you a million pounds, would you sleep with Brad Pitt?" His sister looks up and says, "Omigod! Yes! Definitely!" So Little Johnny goes back to his father. Dad asks, "So has that given you an idea about what 'potential' and 'reality' mean?" "Yes it has," says Little Johnny. "Potentially we could get two million pounds, but in reality we're living with a couple of slappers."

Dad's Excuses For Not Being More Generous

I'm saving to take you all on a holiday of a lifetime (yes, that's right, just the one).

At my age I need to invest more in my private health insurance and, by the way, I'd be a bit healthier if it wasn't for you lot.

You'll get far more when I pop my clogs!

I am thinking of becoming a Buddhist monk and rejecting materialism (mainly because I haven't got any money).

I'm saving to get you through university – the drinks bill alone will cost me an arm and a leg.

I don't want to spoil you.

You won't learn the value of money if you're just handed it on a plate.

You'll only end up paying for my nursing home when I'm old so it's hardly worth handing it over in the first place.

All the best entrepreneurs are self-made, so, if you think about it, I'm actually helping you to become rich by giving you nothing.

If I give you lots of money and mobile phones and Ipods you'll only be a target for muggers.

Religious Education

At a Catholic convent school, one of the nuns asks all the little children in her class what they want to be when they grow up. A little girl puts her hand up and says, "When I grow up, I want to be a prostitute!" "What?" squeals the nun. "That's terrible. That's disgusting. Who put ideas like that in a young child's head? Now I'll ask you one more time, what do you want to do be when you grow up?" "A prostitute," says the little girl. "Oh, a prostitute!" says the nun. "Thank God for that! I thought you said 'a Protestant.'"

A Sunday School teacher was talking to her class about the birth of Christ and she asked the children, "What was Jesus's mother's name?" One child answered, "Mary." The teacher then asked, "And can anyone tell me what Jesus's father's name was?" A little boy said, "Verge." Confused, the teacher asked, "Where did you get that idea from?" The boy said, "Well, you know my dad's a vicar and he's always talking about Verge n' Mary."

A little boy goes to his mother and says, "Mummy, I've got a test at school tomorrow. The teacher's going to ask me 'Who made you?' and I don't know what to say." "Oh, darling," replies his mum. "The answer you should give is 'God made me.' Can you remember that?" Next day the little boy has his test at school and the teacher asks him the question. Unfortunately the little boy has now forgotten what his mother told him and says to the teacher, "Oh dear! Until yesterday I was pretty sure it was my father. But then my mum told me it was actually someone else – and now I've completely forgotten the man's name."

A vicar was greeting the children at his Sunday School, when he noticed little Charlotte. "Why Charlotte," he said. "I understand from your mother that God is sending you a little brother or sister." "Yes," says Charlotte. "And he knows where the money is coming from too. I heard Daddy say so."

At a Catholic school, there was a "meet the teacher" session for the parents and their children. After the meeting, a nun announced that there would be a small reception in the school hall. All the children and parents filed in, and saw on a table a plate of apples, a plate of biscuits and some juice. As the children started to help themselves one boy saw a sign by the apples that said, "Take only one. God is watching." So, the boy took an apple and moved on to the biscuits. He helped himself, and then took a small piece of paper and wrote: "Take all you want. God is watching the apples."

Genuine Extracts From Kids' School Exam Answers and Essays That Should Make Their Dads Proud

A blizzard is when it snows sideways.

A hurricane is a breeze of a bigly size.

Q: Explain how clouds are formed.
A: I am not sure how clouds get formed.
But the clouds know how to do it and that
is the important thing.

A monsoon is a French gentleman.

A vibration is a motion that cannot make up its mind which way it wants to go.

To collect fumes of sulphur, hold a deacon over a flame in a test tube.

Q: How does blood circulate in the human body?
A: Blood flows down one leg and up the other.

Clouds are high-flying fogs.

Clouds just keep circling around the earth. There's not much else to do.

Cyanide is so poisonous that one drop of it on a dog's tongue will kill the strongest man.

For a dog bite, put the dog away for several days. If he has not recovered, then kill it.

A supersaturated solution is one that holds more than it can hold.

The pistol of a flower is its only protection against insects.

Q: How can genetics affect your appearance?
A: Genetics explains why you look like your father, and if you don't, why you should.

For a nosebleed, put the nose much lower than the body until the heart stops.

For asphyxiation, apply artificial respiration until the patient is dead.

For fainting, rub the person's chest, or if a lady, rub her arm above the hand instead. Or put the head between the knees of the nearest doctor.

H2O is hot water and CO2 is cold water.

Henry VIII found walking difficult because he had an abbess on his knee.

Q: Use the word "diploma" in a sentence.
A: Our pipes were leaking so much that my dad called diploma.

Humidity is the experience of looking for air and finding water.

In looking at a drop of water under a microscope, we find there are twice as many Hs as Os.

In some rocks you can find the fossil footprints of fishes.

In the Olympic Games, Greeks ran races, jumped, hurled the biscuits and threw the java.

Q: Give an example of Newton's Third Law of Motion.
A: Hitting someone and they yell "ouch" and hit you back.

Isotherms and isobars are even more important than their names sound.

It is so hot in some places that people there have to live in other places.

You can listen to thunder after lightning and tell how close you came to getting hit. If you don't hear it you got hit, so never mind.

Most books now say our sun is a star. But it still knows how to change back into a sun in the daytime.

Q: Use the word "fascinate" in a sentence.
A: I have a coat with nine buttons but I am only able to fascinate.

John Milton wrote *Paradise Lost*. Then his wife died and he wrote *Paradise Regained*.

Lime is a green-tasting rock.

Litter: a nest of young puppies.

Moses led the Israelites to the Red Sea, where they made unleavened bread, which is bread made without any ingredients. Afterwards, Moses went up on Mount Cyanide to get the Ten Commandments.

Q: Name three kinds of blood vessels.
A: Arteries, vanes and caterpillars.

One of the main causes of dust is DIRT.

Napoleon became ill with bladder problems and was very tense and unrestrained. He wanted an heir to inherit his power, but since Josephine was a baroness, she couldn't bear him any children.

One myth says that the mother of Achilles dipped him in the River Stynx until he became intolerable. Achilles appears in *The Illiad*, by Homer.

Q: What is one horsepower?
A: One horsepower is the amount of energy it takes to drag a horse 500 feet in one second.

One of the main causes of dust is janitors.

Queen Elizabeth was the "Virgin Queen". As a queen she was a success.

Q: Give the meaning of the term "Caesarean Section"?
A: The "Caesarean Section" is a district in Rome.

Queen Victoria was the longest queen. She sat on a thorn for 63 years. She was a moral woman who practised virtue. Her death was the final event which ended her reign.

Rain is often known as soft water, oppositely known as hail.

Rain is saved up in cloud banks.

Rainbows are just to look at, not to really understand.

Sir Francis Drake circumcised the world with a 100-foot clipper. Some oxygen molecules help fires burn while others help make water, so sometimes it's brother against brother.

Some people can tell what time it is by looking at the sun, but I never have been able to make out the numbers.

Q: What is the equator.
A: The equator is a managerie lion running around the Earth through Africa.

Someday we may discover how to make magnets that can point in any direction.

South America has cold summers and hot winters, but somehow they still manage.

Talc is found on rocks and on babies.

The alimentary canal is located in the northern part of Indiana.

The Egyptians lived in the Sarah Dessert and traveled by Camelot. The climate of the Sarah is such that the inhabitants have to live elsewhere, so certain areas of the dessert are cultivated by irritation. The Egyptians built the Pyramids in the shape of a huge triangular cube. The Pyramids are a range of mountains between France and Spain.

Q: What happens to a boy when he reaches puberty?
A: He says goodbye to his boyhood and looks forward to his adultery.

The inhabitants of Egypt were called mummies and they all wrote in hydraulics.

The law of gravity says there's no jumping up without coming back down.

Many dead animals in the past changed to fossils while others preferred to be oil.

Samson slayed the Philistines with the axe of the apostles.

The Jews had trouble throughout their history with unsympathetic Genitals.

The seventh commandment is "Thou shalt not admit adultery".

The word "trousers" is an uncommon noun because it is singular at the top and plural at the bottom.

Paul preached holy acrimony, which is another name for marriage.

**Q: How are the main parts of the
body categorized?
A: The body is consisted into three parts, the
brainium, the borax, and the abdominal cavity. The
branium contains the brain, the borax contains the
heart and lungs, and the abdominal cavity contains
the five bowels A, E, I, O and U.**

The wind is like the air, only pushier.

There are 26 vitamins in all, but some of the letters are yet to be discovered. Finding them all means living forever.

There is a tremendous weight pushing down on the centre of the Earth because of so much population stomping around up there these days.

Thunder is a rich source of loudness.

To most people solutions mean finding the answers. But to chemists solutions are things that are still all mixed up.

**Q: What is water?
A: Melted steam.**

To prevent contraception, use a condominium.

To remove dust from the eye, pull the eye down over the nose.

Vacuums are nothings. We only mention them to let them know we know they're there.

Water freezes at 32 degrees and boils at 212 degrees. There are 180 degrees between freezing and boiling because there are 180 degrees between north and south.

Water vapour gets together in a cloud. When it is big enough to be called a drop, it does.

Q: When did Julius Caesar die?
A: A few days before his funeral.

We keep track of the humidity in the air so we won't drown when we breathe.

When people run around and around in circles we say they are crazy. When planets do it we say they are orbiting.

When they broke open molecules, they found they were only stuffed with atoms. But when they broke open atoms, they found them stuffed with explosions.

Q: Where would you find the world's largest mammals and why?
A: The largest mammals are to be found in the sea because there is nowhere else to put them.

When you breathe, you inspire. When you do not breathe, you expire.

While the earth seems to be knowingly keeping its distance from the sun, it is really only centrificating.

William Tell shot an arrow through an apple while standing on his son's head.

A Dads' Guide To Reading School Reports

So what exactly do all those phrases in the kids' school reports really mean?

A born leader – Runs a protection racket.

Easy-going – Bone idle.

Making good progress – Slightly less awful than last year.

Doesn't seem to be able to concentrate – Obviously sits up half the night watching TV and you are failing as a parent.

Quite a personality – Puts small explosives under teachers' cars and dangles other children from third-floor windows.

Friendly – Never shuts up.

Helpful – Creep.

Reliable – Informs on his friends.

Making progress – At the age of 14 has finally mastered the two times table.

Would benefit from extra tuition – Please send him/her to another school!

Expresses himself confidently – Rude bastard.

Enjoys physical education – A bully.

Has put in a lot of effort this term – A pity about the preceding 12.

Has a promising future in sports – Except perhaps snooker and darts where you have to be able to add up.

Does not accept authority easily – Dad is in prison.

Often appears tired – Insomniac telly addict.

A rather solitary child – He stinks.

Always making the class laugh – Especially when his/her test results are read out.

Has excelled in all subjects – A right little know-it-all who even corrects my spelling and grammar!

University material – A complete shyster who seems to be suffering from a permanent hangover and is only interested in becoming a stand-up comic or a rock star

A pleasure to teach! – Don't worry Dad; you're not likely to ever need a translation for this are you?

Popular in the playground – Sells pornography.

Reports And Results

After his exams are over young Kevin says to his father, "Dad, I failed every single subject apart from algebra." Dad, who isn't exactly surprised, says, "I see, so how did you manage not to fail that then?" Young Kevin replies, "I didn't take it."

A young schoolboy says to his father one day, "Dad, can you write in the dark?" His dad says, "I expect so. Why? What do you want me to write?" The boy answers, "Your name on my school report."

Dad asks his youngest son, "Can I have a look at your school report?" The little boy replies, "No. Sorry. I lent it to my friend tonight because he wanted to use it to scare his mum and dad."

Dad is furious when his son comes home with his school report. "What's this!" yells Dad. "Look at these terrible grades. Little Tommy next door doesn't come home with F's all over his school report!" "I know," says his son. "But it's different for him. He's got clever parents!"

Little Natasha came running into the house after school one day, shouting, "Daddy! Daddy! Guess what? I got a 100 in school today!" "That's fantastic, darling," said her dad. "Come into the living room and tell me all about it." "Well," said Natasha breathlessly, "I got 50 in spelling, 30 in sums and 20 in history..."

A ten-year-old boy came home from school seeming very fed up. "What's the matter, son?" asked his father. "Oh, Dad," said the boy. "It's my marks. They're all wet." "What do you mean, they're all wet?" asked his father. "I mean," said the boy, "they're all below C level."

A student burst into his professor's office and said, "Professor Feinstein, I don't believe I deserve this F you've given me." To which the professor replied, "I agree, but unfortunately it is the lowest grade the University will allow me to give."

The teacher tells Dad, "I can say one thing for definite about your son." "What's that?" asks Dad. "With grades like these," says the teacher, "there's no way he could be cheating."

A little boy comes home from school and says his teacher has given him some career advice. "She said with a mind like mine, I should study criminal law." "That's great, son," says Dad. "So what exactly did she tell you?" "She said I had a criminal mind," says the boy.

Ways In Which Dad May Show The Kids Up At Parent/Teacher Evenings

Ask if there's anywhere he can park his pushbike.

Ask if they have a bar.

Wear his comedy tie with Mickey Mouse on it.

Flirt with a female teacher.

Talk to the caretaker for ten minutes in the belief that he's the teacher.

Dunk his biscuits in his tea and have to fish bits out.

Start doing his Basil Fawlty impression.

Keep pointing out that he pays the teachers' wages through his taxes.

Insist that he has to leave at a certain time, as he doesn't want to miss *Strictly Come Dancing*.

Er, just turn up!

Dad's Guide To Discipline

"I know God knows when you are bad, but it's your parents you have to worry about."
Nine-year-old boy

Never raise a hand to your children; it leaves your groin unprotected.

Dad is really frustrated. He tells his friend, "When I was a little boy, if I did anything wrong, I would be punished by being sent to my room without any dinner. But that's no punishment at all with my son. If I send him to his room he's got his colour TV, CD player and computer all there to enjoy." "So what do you do if he misbehaves?" asks his friend. "There's only one thing I can do," says Dad, " I have to send him to my room."

Dad gets really annoyed when he hears his young son come thundering down the stairs. "OK, Tommy," says Dad "How many more times have I got to tell you to come down the stairs quietly? Now, go back up and come down like a civilized human being." Tommy goes out and a long silence follows until the little boy reappears in the front room. "Now that was very good," says Dad. "I want you to come down the stairs like that every time from now on." "Excellent," says Tommy. "I slid down the banister."

> **"My father established our relationship when I was seven years old. He looked at me and said, 'You know, I brought you into this world and I can take you out. And it don't make no difference to me, I'll make another one look just like you.'"**
>
> **Bill Cosby**

Mum and Dad are so exasperated by their little boy's behaviour they decide to try a religious tack. "How do you think you're ever going to get into Heaven the way you carry on?" they ask. "Easy," says the little boy. "I'll just run in and out and in and out and keep slamming the door and eventually St Peter will tell me, 'Oh for Heaven's sake, Johnny, are you coming in or staying out!'"

Dad's little boy comes home from school looking bruised and battered. "What's happened to you, son?" asks Dad. "You've got a bloody nose, a black eye, a fat lip and your shirt's been torn. Have you been in a fight?" The little boy nods. "Yes," says Dad. "It looks like someone's given you a damn good thrashing." The little boy nods again. "I challenged Tommy to a fight," he explains. "And let him have his choice of weapon." "So what went wrong?" asks Dad. "He chose his sister," says Tommy.

> **"My father used to beat me with his belt... while it was still on him."**
>
> **Zach Galifianakis**

Dad's little boy has been in a fight at school. "I'm really disappointed in you fighting at school," his dad tells him. "How did it all start?" "Well," says the little boy, "he threw a rock at me so I threw one back at him." "That's no good," says Dad. "When he threw the rock at you, what you should have done is come straight to me." "And how would that have helped?" asks the boy. "Well," says Dad, "my aim is a lot better than yours."

> **"If your child is being picked on, or indeed is picking on others, the best thing to do is meet with the other kids' dads, form a men's group and organize a rota whereby all the kids get a turn both at being picked on and at bullying."**
> **Jeremy Hardy**

There is a simple solution to make sure all children are brought up perfectly. All mums and dads should just swap their kids with their next-door neighbours. Because everyone knows exactly how to deal with their neighbour's kids, don't they?

A Kid Knows He's Got Problems When...

After his mum and dad abandoned him as a baby, he was adopted by an organ grinder.

At the age of six he was left an orphan and wondered, "What kind of idiot would leave an orphan to a six-year-old?"

He kept getting left beside the monkey enclosure at the zoo.

He was given a toaster shaped like a rubber duck to play with in the bath.

He was never his mum and dad's favourite, even though he was an only child.

His dad always used to tell him about strange men who would offer him sweets and how he should try and find as many of them as possible.

His dad got a football for him and afterwards told everyone he thought that was a fair swap.

His dad used to play "hide-and-seek" with him and while he counted to 500 his dad went and hid in a different town.

His mum and dad gave him a sandbox to play in for his birthday, but didn't tell him he'd be sharing it with the cat.

His mum and dad gave him his own very special front door key, which turned out to be the key to the local kids' home.

His mum and dad left him on the steps of a police station then handed themselves in.

His mum and dad planned a special, once-in-a-lifetime trip to Disneyland, but didn't take him with them.

His mum and dad threw a "going-into-the-Army" party for him, even though he was only three years old.

His mum and dad told him they had got a magic money box, which he could hide all his pocket money in, but he later discovered this was in fact the coin-operated electric meter.

His mum and dad used to give him his pocket money each week in Traveller's Cheques.

His mum and dad used to take him to orphanages and encourage him to mingle.

His mum and dad used to take him to the zoo, because the animals enjoyed looking at him.

The cat used to be served better food than he was.

When he ran away from home his mum and dad found they weren't able to give the police an accurate description.

When he was a baby, his dad used to throw him up in the air... and then walk briskly away.

When he was born, his dad gave his friend old cigar butts to celebrate.

When his mum cooked him his favourite dinner, she told him this was as a last request.

The Facts Of Life

A sex education class at a junior school was about to begin. Each of the children had had to get a slip signed by their parents to say they agreed with them having the lesson. A little girl hands in her slip and tells the teacher, "My dad says I can take the course as long as there's no homework."

A sweet little girl runs out to the backyard where her father is working and asks him, "Daddy, what's sex?" So, her father sits her down, and tells her all about the birds and the bees. He tells her about conception, sexual intercourse, sperm and eggs etc. He tells her about puberty, menstruation, men and women, and love. He thinks what the hell, and tells her the works, thinking that to tell all is the only way to tell the truth. The girl is somewhat awestruck with this sudden influx of bizarre new knowledge and her father finally asks, "So why did you want to know about sex?" "Oh," she says, "Mummy just said lunch would be ready in a couple of secs..."

One day Mum tells Dad he has to tell their nine-year-old son the facts of life. Reluctantly Dad sits the boy down and begins to tell him about the birds and the bees. "Stop it!" says the boy bursting into tears. "Don't tell me! I don't want to know!" "What's the matter, son?" asks Dad. "We just thought it was best you knew the truth." "No!" says the boy. "When I was six years old you told me there was no such thing as the Easter Bunny, then when I was seven you told me there was no such thing as the Tooth Fairy, at eight you told me there was no Father Christmas, now if you're going to tell me that grown-ups don't have sex, I've got nothing left to live for!"

A farmer dad is helping one of his cows give birth one day. His four-year-old boy wanders into the barn half way through the operation and watches intently. "Wow," says the little boy when the calf finally plops out, "How did that calf get in there?" "Oh great," thinks the Dad to himself. "Now I've got to explain the whole birds and the bees thing to him." "Well," he says to the little boy, "how do you think he got in there?" "I'm not really sure," says his son, "but presumably he must have been going at one hell of a speed when he hit the cow."

American comedian and talk show host Jay Leno recalled how his dad taught him the facts of life: "I was 14. My mother was out of the house... My father called me in. He said, 'The birds and the bees? Do you know about that?' I said, 'I know a little about it.' 'Good, good. How do the Red Sox look? We gonna do it?' And that was it. That was my complete education."

> **"My father told me all about the birds and the bees, the liar – I went steady with a woodpecker 'til I was 21."**
>
> **Bob Hope**

A farmer's little boy goes with his dad to a market. The farmer sees a cow he considers buying and looks at it carefully. He prods it, strokes it and lifts up its tail to give its hind quarters a close examination. "What were you doing there, Dad?" asks the little boy. "Well, you see, son," says the farmer, "you have to do all those things with a cow to see if it's worth buying or not." The next morning the little boy comes running up to his dad and says, "Daddy! Daddy! I just saw Mummy and Uncle Bertie at the back of the barn and do you know what? I think Uncle Bertie's thinking about buying her."

Dads And Teenagers

At every stage of a child's life you're either looking back fondly to times when they were sweet and manageable or forward with keen anticipation to a time when they're a bit more mature. Despite the dire warnings of friends and family you always assume it can't get any worse. Oh, Dad!

Teenagers. They're like mini-adults aren't they? Er no, they're like mini-tornados, mini-Incredible Hulks, mini-disaster zones, mini-plagues of locusts. Who sulk. And slouch. And grunt. Then sulk some more. Just when you think they are beginning to grow up a bit Mother Nature decides, just for a laugh, to inject them full of a seething mass of raging hormones that transforms them into Doctor Jekyll, Mr Hyde, and his totally unhinged axe murderer cousin with an acne complex.

It's bad enough if you have a teenage son, sleeping 'til lunchtime, staying up all night listening to death metal, wearing make-up and eating the entire contents of the fridge every three hours, but if you've got a teenage daughter you've got no chance.

It's been said that men are from Mars and women are from Venus, but what planet are teenage girls from? Planet Get-off-my-case, get-out-of-my-face, you-don't-understand, I-wish-I-were-dead-somewhere-in-some-distant-solar-system? Probably.

If a teenage girl has "women" problems, "boy" problems, or indeed any other type of problem, the last person in the universe she's going to want to discuss it with is Dad. You can consider yourselves pretty privileged parents if she'll discuss them with Mum, so don't worry. It's normal. Just keep your head down for a few years and the teenage stage will pass. Honest.

At his son's 18th birthday party, Dad wasn't too pleased to overhear his son tell a friend, "It's great being 18. Now I can legally do all the things I've been doing since I was 15."

Dad tells his teenage son he needs to start acting a bit more like a grown up. "How can I do that?" says his son. "How can I start to be more independent and self-reliant, and stand on my own two feet, on the miserable allowance you pay me each week."

Pete has just formed his own rock band and his dad tells him one day, "Pete, I wish you and your band could be on TV!" "Wow, Dad!" says Pete really pleased. "You think we're good, eh?" "No," says his dad, "because if you were then I could turn you off!"

Dad can't understand teenagers. He is mystified as to how they can say they don't want to be like anyone else and then all dress exactly the same as each other.

TRUE STORY

A family used to leave notes for themselves stuck to their fridge door. For example, Dad one day stuck up a list of "to dos" including, "Help wife more; lose weight; be more productive at work". The daughter then added another line to the list that read, "Send Catherine money each month." Her brother then added another line, "Make payments on car for Sean." The daughter's boyfriend then chipped in with, "Buy Dave a Jeep." Finally Dad underlines the lot with a brand new goal: "Remember to wean kids."

Dad tells Mum one day, "You know what teenagers are, don't you? They're God's punishment for enjoying sex."

On his 16th birthday Dad tells his son, "You know you're old enough to buy cigarettes now." "That's all right, Dad," says the boy, "I managed to give up three years ago."

Dad's teenage son and his friend are smoking a joint in the local park and get picked up by the police. Down in the cells of the local police station they are told they are entitled to one phone call. Ten minutes later a man turns up to see the desk sergeant. "Ah!" says the sergeant says. "Presumably you're the boys' lawyer." "No," says the man. "I'm here with the pizza they ordered."

Dad says his eldest son has just come back from university with qualifications in sociology, psychology and philosophy. Dad says the lad can't get a job, but the good thing is he knows why.

Dad has some advice for his teenage offspring: "Why don't you leave home now while you still know everything."

Dad's teenage son has decided to start building his body up. Despite reservations about how long this latest fad will last, Dad takes his son to the local sports shop to see the weight lifting equipment. "Are you sure about this?" he asks. "Yes, Dad," says the boy. "I'm going to use them every day." "But they're really expensive," says Dad. "I know," says his son, "but it'll be worth it." "But I know you," says Dad. "You can't usually be bothered doing any hard exercise." "No, Dad," says the boy, "I promise you I've changed this time." So Dad gives in and buys the equipment, holding the door open for his son on their way out. "What?" squeals his son. "You mean I've got to carry them to the car!"

Dad's eldest son reports for a university examination that consists of yes/no questions. He takes his seat in the examination hall, opens the test paper and starts tossing a coin. If he tosses heads, he marks an answer "yes," if it's tails he marks it "no". He finishes the test quickly but spends the time left on re-reading the paper, tossing the coin and occasionally swearing under his breath. The invigilator goes over to see why he's sitting there tossing the coin. "It's OK," says Dad's eldest. "I finished the exam half an hour ago. Now I'm just going through again to check my answers."

Dad's Buzzword Bingo

A fun game for all the family! Simply write down the following phrases on pieces of card and give one each to Mum and the kids. Each time someone hears Dad using one of his well-worn phrases they cross it off the list. The first one to cross off all the phrases on his or her card is declared the winner.

Right! Who's taken my hammer/screwdriver/chainsaw/wind-up torch?

What do you think I am? Made of money?

I need a drink!

I might be a bit late home tonight.

I'll fix this in a jiffy (just before embarking on a two-hour DIY job that never gets completed).

If I'd spoken to my dad like that...

I won't tell you again! (He probably will though).

I'm literally just stopping off for a swift half.

How can I concentrate on driving with that racket going on?

Who's been using my razor to shave their legs?

Are you going to be in that bathroom all day?

As long as you tried your hardest, that's all that matters.

Do what I say, not what I do.

Don't make me come up there!

Don't ask me, ask your mother.

Enough is enough!

I'm spanking you because I love you. This hurts me a lot more than it hurts you.

If I didn't hear it, you didn't say it!

If you don't stop crying, I'll give you something to cry about.

Son, don't ever get married. And tell that to your kids.

This is your last warning.

We'll do it the right way. My way.

When I say no, I mean no.

Why? *Because*, that's why.

When I was your age…

You're going to sit there until you eat your dinner. I don't care if you sit there all night.

You'll realize the value of money once you start earning.

You're certainly not going out dressed like that.

Dad's Guide To Teenage Behaviour And Language

Runs upstairs and slams bedroom door for no apparent reason – onset of puberty.

Takes a sudden interest in the plants in the back garden – has started smoking.

Begs you to buy them a hoodie – first eruptions of acne.

Actually starts what sounds like a polite conversation – wants to borrow the car.

Sleeps 'til three p.m. then eats toast slumped on the sofa until it's time to go "clubbing" – now a fully-fledged teenager.

"Cool!" – a modern translation of your own "yoofspeak" words such as "fab," "groovy" or "wicked".

"Minging!" – a reference to Mum and Dad's dress-sense, household furnishings or cooking.

"ahhnnff!" – OK Dad, whatever you say.

"Uh?" – I'm sorry Father, you are speaking in plain English and I have no idea what you are talking about."

"Daa–aad?" – the preface to a long drawn-out demand for money.

Dads In History

Lady Godiva's dad

Lady Godiva was about to go out of the front door one day
wearing a rather revealing dress when Mr Godiva said, "Oi,
young lady, you're not going out dressed like that!" So she
didn't.

John Logie Baird's dad

Mr Baird senior was worried about young John, a shy and
withdrawn child, who would spend hours just staring at the
living room wall. "Look son," he would say. "This isnae healthy,
get oot in the yard and play fitba or something. Or if you're too
bone idle to do that at least you could invent television or some
such to watch instead of staring at the wall." Young John was
thus inspired to produce an electronic contraption that would
soon rival staring at the wall as a method for wasting young lives.

Nell Gwynn's dad

Mr Gwynn warned young Eleanor (for that was her real name)
never to let a gentleman squeeze her oranges unless he was
intending to pay for them. Good advice Dad! She managed to
stay out of the clutches of ne'er do wells and ended up having a
child by fruity old King Charles II.

Attila The Hun's dad

Attila's mother had always wanted a girl so would dress little
"Tilly" as she nicknamed him in pretty dresses with pink ribbons
in his long hair. She had had visions of her daughter going into

the church and becoming Attila the Nun, but when young Tilly grew up and started sprouting facial hair at an alarming rate his dad decided enough was enough. "He looks a right plonker with eye make-up and a five o'clock shadow. I'm going to bring him up the right way!" He went to the nearest branch of Weapons R Us and kitted young Tilly out with the most fearsome armoury imaginable, with which he then attempted to take over the world. Nice one, Dad.

Florence Nightingale's dad

When young Florence was growing up she had a single-minded ambition to go into the health service, but her father would plead, "All right love, you want a career, fair enough, but for crying out loud, not nursing! The pay's terrible, you've got no career path and then there's MRSA…" Did she listen? Do girls ever listen to their dads?

Michelangelo's dad

Mr di Lodovico Buanarotti (whew, no wonder Michaelangelo only ever used his first name!) despaired of his son wandering around Tuscany in a hoodie scribbling on walls. "Alora!" He would exclaim, "Yer think you're clever do you, scribbling on folks' walls? Well if you're so bloomin' clever try scribbling on the ceiling. With a bit of luck you'll fall off yer ladder and it'll teach you a lesson." Sadly it didn't and ever since then the habit of scribbling on walls (and ceilings) has been known by the Italian word "graffiti" in honour of young Mick.

Boudicca's dad

What are little girls made of? Sugar and spice and all things nice? Not this one baby! Dad had wanted a son and made the tragic mistake of giving her clubs and battleaxes instead of dolls and teddies. She went on to lead a gang known as the Iceni or the East Anglia massive and gave some Italian illegal immigrants a hard time.

You Really Know You're A Dad When...

You only go to nightclubs to collect your teenage kids.

"A drink with the boys" means sharing fizzy pop with your male offspring.

The last time you played 18 holes was taking your kids round a crazy golf course.

You only stay up late when the baby won't go to sleep.

Your idea of self–indulgence is finishing off the kids' leftover chips.

Even your wife calls you Dad.

You get all the way to work before discovering baby food down your tie.

You know all the words to the *Postman Pat* song.

You can name all four members of the *Teletubbies* and what colour suits they wear.

Half your birthday presents are homemade.

You find yourself second in command with the TV remote control.

On Mother's Day you're suddenly buying for two.

You're allowed to go on the playground swings again without people thinking you're a loony.

Your credit card is out more than you are.

Dad's Bounteous Gifts For All The Family

Dad asks his eldest son, "Son, what would you like for your birthday?" "Not much," says the boy. "Just a radio... with a sports car round it!"

It's mid December and Dad is sitting reading the newspaper when his little boy pops his head round the living room door. "Dad, you'll have to get in touch with Father Christmas quick and tell him to bring me a different present, because I don't want a bike any more." "Oh really," says Dad. "Why not?" "Because," says the little boy, "I've just found a bike exactly like the one I asked for hidden at the back of our garage."

> **"Christmases were terrible, not like nowadays when kids get everything. My sister got a miniature set of perfumes called Ample. It was tiny, but even I could see where my dad had scraped off the S..."**
> **Stephen K Amos**

Dad takes his three children to spend the night at their grandparents one weekend. He reminds them to say their prayers as he gets them settled in the spare room and kneels down to say his own prayers (thanking the Good Lord for his wonderful life as a dad and for having been blessed with a family who have made sure he never has to worry about what to spend his money on). He is climbing into bed himself when he is shocked to hear the kids shouting their prayers at the tops of their voices: "I PRAY FOR NEW ROLLER BLADES!" "I PRAY FOR A NEW NINTENDO!" "I PRAY FOR A NEW DOLL'S HOUSE!" Dad goes into the spare room and tells them off. "For goodness sake there's no need to shout your prayers! God isn't deaf!" "We know that," says the eldest one. "But Grandma and Grandad are!"

As Dad knows to his cost, the most effective way to make sure you always remember Mum's birthday is to forget it just the once.

> **"I never know what to give anyone for their birthday. Last year I just gave my dad a hundred dollars and said, "Go and buy me something that will make your life easier." He went out and bought a present for my mother."**
> **Rita Rudner**

It was close to Fathers' Day and Mum was taking her four-year-old daughter to the shop to find a nice card for Daddy. She showed her the rack of cards for dads and told her to choose one while she looked for a present. When she turned back, the little girl was picking up one card after another, opening them up and quickly shoving them back into the rack, making it look untidy. "Darling, what are you doing?" she asked. "Haven't you found a nice card for Daddy yet?" "No," she said. "I'm looking for one of the ones that has money in it."

A father had identical twin daughters, but although they looked exactly alike their personalities were poles apart. One liked broccoli, one hated it; if one said a room was too hot, the other would say it was too cold. If one said the television was too loud, the other would say she couldn't hear it properly. Plus, one was an eternal optimist, the other a terrible pessimist. So, just to test them out one Christmas Eve, Dad filled the pessimist's room with piles of toys, presents and games, while he dumped a huge pile of horse manure in the optimist's room. On Christmas morning he heard loud sobbing coming from the pessimist's room. "What's up darling?" Dad asked. "Because I've got so many toys I don't know which one to play with first, and all my friends will be jealous, and I haven't got enough cupboard space to keep them, and Mum will get annoyed because my room's a mess, and..." So Dad sympathized and then went into her sister's bedroom where the eternal optimist was grinning all over and looking through the big pile of horse manure. "You look happy," he said, surveying the scene. "How come you're so delighted by this big pile of horse manure?" "Oh, Daddy," said the little girl, "I'm just so thrilled because I know there's got to be a pony in here somewhere!"

My mum told me the best time to ask my dad for anything was during sex. Not the best advice I'd ever been given. I burst in through the bedroom door saying, "Can I have a new bike?" He was very upset. His secretary was surprisingly nice about it. I got the bike.

Jimmy Carr

A few days before her birthday a husband asked his wife, "Dear, what would you like for your present?" His wife said, "I really don't think I should say." Her husband said, "How about a diamond ring?" But his wife said, "I'm not really all that keen on diamonds." "All right then," said her husband. "How about a nice mink coat?" "You know I don't agree with wearing fur," said his wife. "OK, then, how about a gold necklace?" said hubby. "I've got three of them already," said his wife. "Well, blimey," said the husband. "What on Earth do you want?" "What I'd really like," said his wife, "is a divorce." "Oh you don't do you?" said the husband. "I wasn't really planning on spending that much."

A forester had raised his only son and had managed to finance the young man's university education the only way he knew how, by cutting down trees by hand. The young man had helped his father and knew how hard his father had worked to put him through university. When the son started university he promised himself the first thing he would do would be to buy his father a present that would make the old man's life easier. The son saved and scrimped and finally had enough money to purchase the finest chainsaw in the world. On a school holiday the son asked his dad how many trees he could cut down in one day. The father, a large burly man, thought and said on a good day he was able to bring down 20 trees. The son gave the father the brand new chainsaw and said from now on he would be able to triple the amount and only work half as hard. The old man was very pleased and said he had the best son in the world. The young man left for university the next morning and wasn't able to return until the next break, three months later. When he arrived he immediately noticed that his dad appeared very tired and run down. He asked if his father was feeling all right. The old man replied that cutting trees was getting harder and harder, and now with the new chainsaw he was working longer hours, but not cutting as many trees as before. The son knew there was something wrong and thought perhaps the saw he purchased wasn't as good as advertised. He asked to check it out. He took the chainsaw, checked the oil and found that was full. He checked the petrol and that too was full. He yanked on the cord and immediately the chainsaw roared to life. His father grabbed him by the shirt and shouted, "WHAT THE HELL'S THAT NOISE!!!!"

Dad Stereotypes

When you become a dad you have to decide which sort you're going to be. Here are a few of the options:

Trad dad

You not only bring home the bacon, you expect it to be sitting on the table, cooked, when you get home too. You rule the house with a rod of iron and possibly smoke a pipe in your spare time. You have certain unwritten rules: Dad has to read the newspaper before anyone else; Dad does not get involved in ironing, washing or cooking; children should be seen and not heard (and preferably not seen as well); if it was good enough for my dad it's good enough for me.

Likely children's names: Muriel, Timothy

Lad dad

Suddenly finds he has become a parent one day when he wasn't paying attention and now has to help bring up a child in between going to the pub, watching the footy and playing computer games.

Likely children's names: Paris, Brooklyn

Mad dad

His sense of humour has never deserted him even though half his family probably have if they've got any sense. Likes a laugh and a joke, though not necessarily in that order. Pretends to shake hands with children and thumbs his nose, tells jokes that a Christmas cracker manufacturer would turn his nose up at, and has own supply of whoopee cushions, "mucky pup" poo and stink bombs.

Likely children's names: Lulu, Hercules

Bad dad

Ducks and dives, dodges and weaves, wheels and deals like some renegade left over from *Minder*. Been in and out of nick more times than a prison laundry van, but "luvs his kids to bits". Probably sees more of them than many dads because he "works nights, know what I mean?"

Likely children's names: 'chelle, Ronnie

Sad dad

Often seen wearing a pinny and rubber gloves. Is more familiar with the U-bend than the G-spot and embarrasses children by coming over all mum-like at the school gates, hanky-dabbing faces and straightening ties, etc. Probably watches *Richard and Judy*.

Likely children's names: India, Josh

Songs About Dads

"Daddy Cool" – Darts

"Daddy Cool" – Boney M

"My Heart Belongs To Daddy" – Eartha Kitt

"Daddy's Home" – Cliff Richard

"Daddy Don't You Walk So Fast – Daniel Boone

"Daddy's Little Girl" – Nicky D

"Papa's Got a Brand New Bag" – James Brown

"Papa's Got a Brand New Pigbag" – Pigbag

"Papa Don't Preach" – Madonna

"Papa Loves Mama" – Joan Regan

"Papa Loves Mambo" – Perry Como

"Papa Oom Mow Mow" – The Trashmen

"Papa Was A Rolling Stone" – The Temptations

"Poppa Joe" – Sweet

"Poppa Piccolino" – Diana Decker

"Pops We Love You" – Diana Ross, Marvin Gaye, Smokey Robinson, Stevie Wonder

"Father" – Christians

"Father" – LL Cool J

"Father and Son" – Boyzone

"Father Figure" – Gorge Michael

"Father Christmas Do Not Touch Me" – The Goodies

Dads And Daughters

Yes, having a teenage daughter is pretty tough for a dad, but then it's pretty tough for dads with daughters of any age. At the risk of stating the obvious, daughters are women. Hold that thought in your head as you bring them up and you can't go far wrong. Well you probably will go wrong, but at least you'll know why.

You are incompatible. You want to get her interested in football, she'll stay interested in dolls – at least until she's old enough to fancy a footballer and have a poster of him on her bedroom wall. Then you'll wish she were interested in dolls again.

Try as you might you will probably find it impossible to get fully engaged in admiring the layout of her dolls' house, discussing the finer points of netball or which boy band member is the most, like, totally gorgeous. And, as stated above, you will not have the foggiest idea what she is going through as a teenager. Though you'd think that as she starts to get interested in boys you'd have some sort of mutual ground to explore; after all you were a boy once, you used to go out with teenage girls. You understand what it's all about don't you? Precisely! And that's why you and she will be at permanent loggerheads over boys for the foreseeable future.

Even when she gets married you won't fully welcome her chosen partner into the family until he joins your pub darts team. By that time he'll probably be a dad too and the two of you will be allies in the never-ending battle against women.

Dad's two daughters are given parts in the nativity play at their primary school. At dinner that night, they argue because when they both think they've been given the most important role.

Finally the ten-year-old says, "Well you can just ask Mummy which is the better role. I know for a fact she'll say it's much harder to be a virgin than it is to be an angel."

Dad's ten-year-old brings home her school report. Her marks are all very good, but at the bottom is a note from her teacher saying that while she is a clever girl, she talks far too much in class. "I have an idea I am going to try," says the teacher, "which I think may rid her of the habit." Dad signs the report and sends it back with a note that says, "Please let me know if your idea works on my daughter, because if it does I would really like to try it out on her mother."

TRUE STORY

One day a man was out in his car with his four-year-old daughter and beeped his car horn by mistake. She turned and looked at him for an explanation. He said, "I did that by accident." She replied, "I know you did, Daddy." "How did you know that?" asks the dad. "Because," said the little girl, "you didn't shout 'arsehole' out of the window afterwards!"

Any father will tell you that dads spend the first three years of their daughter's life trying to get them to speak and then the next 15 trying to get them to shut up again.

The phone rings, Dad's teenage daughter answers and then settles down and natters away for the next hour before finally hanging up. "Wow," says Dad. "That was a short conversation for you. What happened?" "It was a wrong number," she says.

In 2002, Rolling Stone Mick Jagger discovered that his 18-year-old daughter, Elizabeth, was going out with a 44-year-old man.

Although Mick himself had often gone out with women who were more than 25 years his junior, he nevertheless went ballistic (allegedly).

Two young girls are talking about their boyfriends. "I've got a real problem," says the first. "Every time I take a boy home to meet my parents, my Dad tells me he doesn't approve of him." "Well," says her friend, "why don't you try and find a boy who's just like your Dad?" "Oh I've tried that one," says the first girl. "What happened?" asks the other. "My Mum couldn't stand him."

Dad's eldest daughter wants to get married. Being a traditionalist her fiancé asks Dad for her hand in marriage. Afterwards she asks, "What did Dad say when you asked for his permission to marry me?" "He didn't say much actually," says the young man. "He just sobbed gently to himself for a while and then looked up and started shouting, 'Thank you, God! Thank you!'"

Rebecca brings the boy she wishes to marry home to meet her parents. Dad invites the young man into his study and asks him a few questions. "So, Joseph," he says. "What are your plans in life?" Joseph, a good Jewish boy, tells him, "I'm a scholar of the Torah." "Very good," says Dad. "But what are you going to do to keep my daughter in the style to which she is accustomed?" "I will study and God will surely provide for us," says Joseph. "OK," says Dad, "but will you be able to afford to buy her a decent engagement ring?" "I will study hard," says Joseph, "and God will provide for us." "Right," says Dad, "and what about children? How will you support a family?" "Don't worry, sir," says Joseph. "God will provide." A little while later Mum asks Dad what he found out about their daughter's fiancé. "Well," says Dad, "he has no job, no plans and no prospects, but the good news is – he thinks I'm God!"

TRUE STORY

A mum was out walking with her four-year-old daughter when she picked something up off the ground and went to put it in her mouth. The mum stopped her. "What's the matter?" asked the little girl. "Well," said the mum, "that's been lying on the ground so it's dirty. It's probably covered in germs." "Wow!" said the little girl. "How do you know that kind of thing?" "Erm," said the mum, trying to think of a good answer, "that's because it's on the mummy test. You have to learn all those kind of things before they'll let you be a mummy." "OK," said the little girl as she took this in, "and if you fail the test, you have to be a daddy instead. Right?" "Yes, that's correct," said the mum.

Mum is anxiously waiting at the airport. Her daughter has been away for six months travelling around the world seeking adventure. During this time it seems she has met the perfect man, and gone straight ahead and married him. Eventually Mum sees her coming through customs, but walking alongside her is a man dressed in feathers, covered with exotic markings and carrying a grotesque shrunken human head. The daughter cheerfully introduces her new husband and hopes her mum will be pleased, because he's exactly the sort of man she advised her to marry. "No, you idiot," hisses Mum in her ear. "I told you to marry a rich doctor! A RICH doctor!"

Dad's Dictionary

Amnesia: The condition that may one day enable a woman who has been through labour to have sex again

Baby: Potential future golf partner if boy or future ally of Mum in war against Dad if girl

Babysitter: Passport to pub

Cooker: Mum (if, that is, the family want something edible at dinner time)

Dishwasher: Mum (according to Dad while he's down the pub, but not while he's at home if he knows what's good for him)

DIY: Jobs done by Dad then later re-done by professional on Mum's instruction while Dad's out at work

Double bed: Piece of bedroom furniture with a husband on one side, a wife on the other and an argument in the middle

Family car: Run by Dad, run into ground by the rest of family

Household budget: Planned expenditure which has no relation whatsoever to actual expenditure

Independent: How Mum and Dad want their children to be as long as they do everything they're told

Intuition: The strange instinct that tells Mum she's right, whether she is or not. (Thanks, Oscar!)

Iron: Piece of golfing equipment

Marriage: An institution, a bit like Bedlam

Ow: The first word spoken by children with older siblings

School: Free babysitting service

Shed: Place of refuge so inhospitable to women that you will be left in peace there

Speech: The ability to whine in words

Sterilize: What you do to your first baby's dummy by boiling it and to your most recent baby's dummy by blowing on it

Top bunk: Place where you should never put a child wearing Superman pyjamas

Wages: Semi-mythical entity that only exists on paper and has no physical existence

Whodunit: None of the kids that live in your house obviously

Work: A sanctuary from family life

Differences Between Boys And Girls – A Guide For New Dads

You throw a little girl a ball and it will hit her in the nose. You throw a little boy a ball and he will try to catch it. Then it will hit him in the nose.

Even at an early age girls are attracted to boys. Boys, on the other hand, are attracted to dirt.

Most baby girls talk before boys do. Before boys talk, they learn how to make machine-gun noises.

Girls will cry if someone dies in a film. Boys will cry if you turn off the DVD after they've watched *Star Wars* three times in a row.

Girls turn into women. Boys turn into bigger boys.

Boys' rooms are usually messy. Girls' rooms are usually messy, but at least it's a nice smelling mess.

A girl will pick up a stick and look in wonderment at what nature has made. A boy will pick up a stick and hit his sister with it.

When girls play with Barbie and Ken dolls, they like to dress them up and play "mummies and daddies" with them. When boys play with Barbie and Ken dolls, they like to tear off their limbs.

Boys couldn't care less if their hair is unruly. Girls would rather lock themselves in their room for two weeks than be seen in public with a haircut that went wrong.

Baby girls find Mummy's makeup and instinctively start painting their face. Baby boys find Mummy's makeup and instinctively start painting the walls.

If a girl accidentally burps, she will be embarrassed. If a boy accidentally burps, he will follow it with a dozen fake ones.

Boys grow their fingernails long because they're too lazy to cut them. Girls grow their fingernails long – not because they look nice – but because they can dig them into a boy's arm.

Indications That Dad May Not Entirely Trust His Daughter's New Boyfriend

He suddenly presents her with a chastity belt.

He gets the local police to run a CRB check.

He tells the boyfriend that his daughter has a contagious disease and warns him not to go near her under any circumstances.

He answers the door to the new boyfriend casually carrying a shotgun under his arm.

He tells the boy his daughter has chronic agoraphobia and he can't take her out of the house.

He pretends he's not her father, but her husband.

He tells the boyfriend that, despite the fact his daughter is a fully qualified solicitor, she is still not 16.

He will only let the boyfriend take her out in his car if he buys one without a back seat.

He installs CCTV in her bedroom.

He warns his daughter that the boy is just like he was at the same age.

What Dad Says About His Daughter's New Boyfriend — And What He Really Means

Big lad isn't he? – I'd better make sure I'm armed if I have to throw *him* out of the house.

Hasn't got a lot to say for himself has he? – Does he speak English by any chance?

Seems like a nice enough bloke – What's the catch?

What's he do for a living? – Can I get him to do some building work/show me how to work my computer/service the car for nothing?

Seems a very confident young man – Flash little git!

He wouldn't have been my first choice for you – I'll be watching him like a hawk.

Bit of a character isn't he? – He's had more tattoos than the Black Watch band!

Where did you meet him? – Where on earth did you find him?!

We'll have to invite him over for dinner one evening – Do you want to book the church or shall I?

Have you met his parents yet? – I bet he lives in a squat.

His Daughter's Boyfriends – Dad's Worst Nightmares

She brings home a hulking hairy, tattooed monster with piercings all over his face.

She then says she wants to marry him.

She brings home someone who earns more than he does and still expects him to pay for the wedding.

She refers to her boyfriends as "Monday," "Tuesday," etc.

She goes out with the meanest, hardest looking head case in the district and then dumps him after the first date.

After a polite conversation about Dad's business affairs she casually reveals that the new boyfriend works for the Inland Revenue and is really keen for promotion.

She finally meets the son of a millionaire – but he's just become a hippy and renounced all worldly possessions to doss on people's floors instead.

The first thing the boyfriend does when he's introduced is challenge Dad to an arm-wrestling competition.

When asked what she likes about him she replies: "He doesn't smoke and he doesn't drink – well at least not since he joined this religious cult…"

You vaguely recognize him from a newspaper Photofit picture.

Quotes From Great Dads Of The World – Jim Royle

Denise: Dad, stop fiddling with yourself.
Jim: I'm not fiddling with meself, I paid a quid for these underpants and I've got about 50 pence worth stuck up me arse.

Nana: May God forgive you, Jim, for talking ill of the dead like that.
Jim: I wasn't speaking ill of the dead, I was speaking about you, the living bloody dead!

Jim: Woah-ho, if you lot take my advice, you won't go near that lavatory for at least half an hour and whatever you do don't strike a bloody match.

Jim: One greedy, scrounging git that fella. What a bloody brass neck! Coming back here for his Sunday dinner!
Dave: You asked him Jim!
Jim: I know… but I didn't think he'd say, "Yes!"

Jim: (Talking about Nana) Thinks the bloody world of me? Today she had a family size bag of bloody Revels, and did she offer me one? Did she shite! She sat on her fat arse, announcing every one as she put it in her big fat gob. Oooh, coconut, oooh orange, ooooh Malt-bloody-teasers.

Nana: Eh, I tell you who is in hospital, Gwen's husband.
Barbara: Ooh, what's he having done?
Nana: He's having something fitted.
Jim: What – a wardrobe?

Nana: Is this hat too far forward?
Jim: No, we can still see your face.

Antony: Who's stunk that toilet out?
Barbara: Who d'ya think.
Jim: Well that's what it's for isn't it, where d'you expect me to sh*t? You'd soon have something to worry about if I crapped in the kitchen.

Denise: Will you stop talking about Nana dying?
Jim: Yeah! Have a little bit of respect – wait 'til she's gone out of the door. Oh, I'm only joking, Norma – bloody hell, it'll be a sad day in this house when you snuff it... if we don't get that clock.

Jim: I'm gonna go and have a chat with the Arabs.
Cheryl: What d'ya mean Jim?
Jim: Mustapha Crap.

Dads And Cars

If an Englishman's home is his castle then a dad's car is his chariot.

Women assume that once you have a family then the car is some sort of extension of the home, complete with cuddly toys, food provisions, baby seats and mobile medical supplies.

For most dads this is a complete travesty. Does Lewis Hamilton have a "Baby on board" sticker on the back of his Formula One job? Would Michael Schumacher have a sunscreen shaped like a cat on his side window? Would even Mr Bean want to sing along to "The Wheels on the Bus" as he drove along? No, no, and probably no.

But there you are. You have the kids, you have to face the consequences and if your cherished motor now looks like a mobile branch of Toys R Us then it's your tough Donald Duck.

This is maybe why so many mums drive those big scary looking 4x4s. If the car looked on the outside as it did on the inside – all fluffy bunnies and primary colours – it would be driven off the road by other contemptuous road users in five seconds flat, but when it looks like a Chieftain tank with attitude even bus drivers think twice about taking it on.

> **"Some people argue that the car is a substitute phallus and this explains men's aggressive driving. But if this were so, why would men drive too fast? Surely they would just back in and out of the garage – or maybe just polish the car a lot."**
>
> **Jeremy Hardy**

One day in a chemistry lesson at school, the teacher asks his class, "Can anyone tell me what happens to a car when it gets old and starts to rust." "Yes," says one little boy. "My dad buys it."

Dad says his car has been up and down on the hydraulic lift at the local garage so often it's one of the few cars around that has done a higher mileage vertically than horizontally.

> **"Men like cars, women like clothes. Women only like cars because they take them to clothes."**
>
> **Rita Rudner**

Dad's kids can't believe he's never bothered to get a stereo system fitted in his car, but he says he's already got a perfectly good one: Mum in the passenger seat and her mother in the back.

Dad arrives home from work to find Mum looking very solemn and his eldest son looking rather shaken up and bruised. "I've got good news and bad news about the car," says Mum. "OK," says Dad. "Tell me the good news first." "Well," says Mum, "the air bag definitely works."

Dad comes home and his son tells him he's taken the car out and now he can't get it to start. "What's happened?" asks Dad. "I think it might be water in the carburettor," says his son. "Really?" says dad. "What makes you think that?" "I accidentally drove it into the canal," says the boy.

Mum reverses the car out of the garage and manages to do £2,000 worth of damage in the process. The reason: Dad had reversed the car into the garage a few minutes earlier.

Dad's son has an accident in the car one day. "What happened?" asks Dad. "It was a nightmare," says the boy. "I had to swerve to avoid a tree, but no matter how far I swerved there was the tree still right in front of me." "You idiot," says Dad. "That wasn't a tree. That was the air freshener."

Dad asks Mum why there are so many dents on the driver's side of her car. "The brakes must be bad on that side," says Mum.

Dad gets fed up with Mum's driving. In the end he tries to make her more careful by frightening her. He tells her that if she has an accident and it's reported in the local paper, they will print her real age.

> **"The other day I got pulled over for speeding. The officer said, 'Don't you know the speed limit is only 55 miles an hour?' I said, 'Yeah, I know, but I'm not going to be out that long.'"**
> **Steven Wright**

Dad's eldest son is taking another lesson. The instructor asks him, "What would you do if you were going up an icy hill and the engine stalled and the brakes failed?" The boy replies, "I'd quickly adjust the rear view mirror."

Dad is incensed one day when he finds someone has bashed into his car. His faith in human nature is, however, revived when he sees a handwritten note left under the windscreen wiper. He unfolds it and reads, "There is a policeman standing across the road watching me while I write you this note. He thinks I'm going to leave you my name, address and insurance details. But I'm not. PS. Sorry for wrecking your car."

Dad asks his idiot teenage son to go round to the back of the car and check if his rear indicator light is working properly. The teenager adopts a pose of great concentration and a moment later Dad hears, "Yes it's working... no, it's stopped... it's working again... no. Yes... no..."

Dad gets his son to wash his car for him. "Hey, is this Turtle Wax stuff really expensive?" says the boy. "Yes, it is," says Dad "That's because turtles have really small ears."

Dad has the bonnet of his car up when a tramp walks past. The tramp stops and peers in. "Piston broke," explains Dad. "Ah yes," says the tramp. "Exactly the same as me then."

Dad once told his son, "You know, you never really learn to swear until you learn to drive."

Dad is driving along down a narrow country lane one day when he graciously pulls into the side of the road to allow a lady driver coming along in the opposite direction to go past him. As she passes Dad's car, the lady winds down her windows and shouts, "Pig!" Dad is incensed. "Bitch!" he yells after her, then shoots off round the next bend where he crashes straight into a pig.

> **"I'm in no condition to drive... Wait! I shouldn't listen to myself, I'm drunk!"**
> **Homer Simpson**

The office where Dad works has finally come up with a way to make sure all 100 of its employees are in work on time each morning. They've reduced the number of spaces in the company car park to 80.

Dad takes his teenage son to the Motor Show one year. The pair split up to look around and when they meet again the son is looking a bit disappointed, because the cars weren't as new as he'd expected. "You idiot!" says Dad. "You've just spent the past eight hours walking round the car park, haven't you?"

Dad's eldest son is out on a driving lesson. His instructor tells him, "OK. When we start going up this next hill I think you'd better change gear." "What?" says the boy? "I didn't know I had to bring a different outfit."

An Inventory Of Minor Damage Caused To Dad's Car Over The Years

Teeth marks in rear seat belt – this is what happens when you forget to bring the baby's teething ring with you, isn't it?

The back seat of many colours – a kaleidoscopic patina resulting from spills of juice, milk, broken glow sticks, nail varnish, glitter, face paint, vomit and a thousand other unmentionables.

Smudgy windows – a result of many years of rubbing out mist drawings, fixing sun screen suction pads and various stickers saying "Baby on board" or "Apoplectic dad on board" etc.

Irremovable mud – the floor in the back looks as though Jonny Wilkinson and the boys have just played an international rugby match in here, and despite a weekly going over with the J Edgar, it never looks any better.

Wobbly rear-view mirror – after years of swivelling it trying to keep an eye on the kids in the back, rather than the more pressing issue of articulated lorries getting too close for comfort, not to mention Mum or teenage daughters applying make-up, the RVM is now held up with gaffer tape.

Minor scrapes to boot – incurred by small children insisting on being allowed to "drive" the supermarket trolley back to the car.

Cigarette burns in back seat – mysteriously appeared after teenager, who apparently doesn't smoke, borrowed the car for the evening.

Musty-smelling seats – never quite recovered after children insisted on washing the car one weekend, but failed to notice the sunroof was open at the time.

Various interior knocks and scrapes – good news/bad news when kids asked to hoover out the car, but took off more than the dirt.

Minor damage to rear window and bumper – following daughter's wedding and various humorous objects being affixed to back of car.